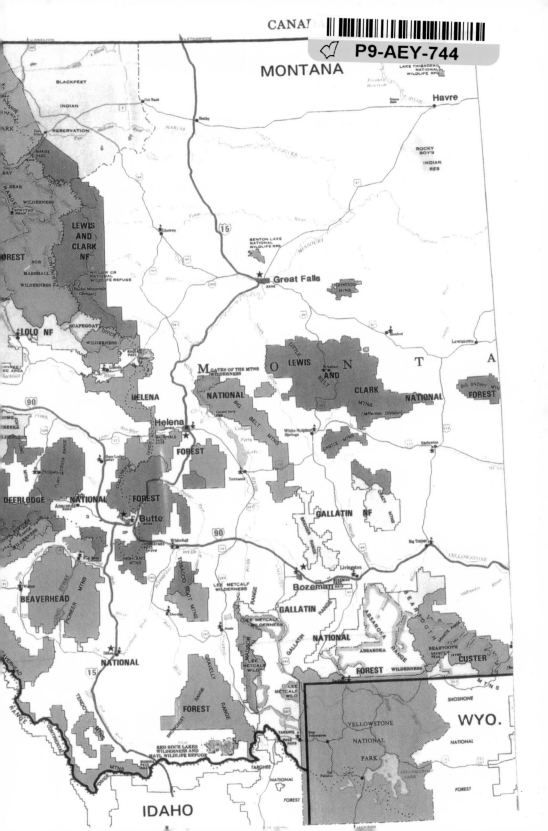

Praise for SMOKEJUMPERS, '49
BROTHERS IN THE SKY
by Starr Jenkins
with photos by Peter Stackpole:

"As one who was there in 1949, I think your book is an outstanding presentation of how it really was. The photographs brought back the old excitement . . . and your stories . . .were excellent and probably typical [of the experiences] for most of us . . . I know that your book will be well received by those of us who were there and . . . by people in the general public who are interested in firefighting, smokejumping, mountain flying and aviation history."
Robert W. Sallee, only living survivor of the Mann Gulch Fire.

"I enjoyed your book very much . . . It portrays the jumper experience very well . . . There is no question but that jumpers will enjoy your book, and I hope many other folks as well."
H. W. "Skip" Stratton, leader of the body-retrieval crew after the Mann Gulch Fire.

"This book moves at an excellent pace and is a handsome one---writer and photographer well-matched. And your writing is full of the energy and spirit these narratives deserve . . . .
"What moved me most were the sections about your brother---the fine letters, the tragic end. I must have known that you, too, lost a brother in his youth, but I had forgotten. Reading your book made him very much alive. You have created a fine tribute to him."
Anita Navon, retired staff member, Hoover Institution, Stanford, and sister of ex-paratrooper Dave Navon, victim of Mann Gulch.

SMOKEJUMPERS, '49
BROTHERS IN THE SKY

By Starr Jenkins

With photographs by PETER STACKPOLE

MERRITT STARR BOOKS
San Luis Obispo
California

Published in the United States of America by
Merritt Starr Books
P.O. Box 1165
San Luis Obispo, CA 93406

Order additional copies from your bookstore
or directly from the address above.

Unless otherwise noted, all photographs in
this volume are by Peter Stackpole.

ISBN 1-886659-09-5
Library of Congress Catalog Card Number:
95-94011

In memory of Dave Navon:
paratrooper, forester,
smokejumper, friend.

CONTENTS

How This Book Came to Be

This book was born because of another great LIFE photographer, Mark Kauffman. For six years starting in 1986, Mark taught photography at Cal Poly, San Luis Obispo, until the massive budget cuts of 1992 forced his department to retire him a second time. The smitten school couldn't keep on their payroll a world class photographer who had made his first cover of LIFE with the most beautiful shot ever made of Eleanor Roosevelt when he was just seventeen. But to honor this legendary lensman the Art Department asked him to put on a retrospective show of his work. This he did, spectacularly, and a marvelous show it was---entitled <u>A Slice of LIFE</u>. To honor him on this occasion six or a dozen of his LIFE colleagues and former editors came from all over the country to help Mark put on a pre-show lecture, talk-fest, slide show and movie-clip demonstration. For two hours the standing-room audience was rapt.

One of these distinguished visitors was Peter Stackpole, a great LIFE photographer who got his start shooting stills and film clips of the building of the San Francisco Bay Bridge and the Golden Gate Bridge in 1934 through l937. He got right up there with the workmen, the bridgemen, hanging on cables and crawling up those immense towers. Incredible pictures. He showed at Mark's show a brief film of these historic feats called The Bridgemen, a wonderful film narrated by then San Francisco Mayor Dianne Feinstein. That film alone would secure Peter's place in the history of photography. As each distinguished guest took his turn Mark told a little about each one, including the fact that Peter was soon to bring out a new Stackpole photo book on Hollywood and the stars he had photographed between 1936 and 1952. [Now published as Life in Hollywood: l936-l952.]

One in that admiring Cal Poly audience was I. In fact I had come especially to see Peter Stackpole---since 43 years before, in the summer of 1949, I had seen him as a young LIFE photographer shooting hundreds of photos of our smokejumper crew---training, flying and jumping out of airplanes in and around Missoula, Montana. And I had even shot a few photos of Peter himself as he worked setting up shots of smokejumpers in front of the old Ford Trimotor aircraft, or the slightly newer DC-3---photos he took around the old Hale Field, and among the jumpers at our training camp at Ninemile. And near the end of the job I believe Dave Navon was with me when we encountered Peter on the steps of the Post Office in Missoula; Peter had 2 or 3 shoeboxes of undeveloped film (his whole 3 weeks of work) wrapped up for mailing back to LIFE in New York. That was how it was done working for the mightiest picture-weekly of all time. The editors would see the finished pictures, enlarged, way before the photographer would have any chance to see them, or cull them, let alone have the chance to crop, enlarge, or bring out the best through darkroom magic. And the editors would make up the story layout from the pictures they liked, cropping or shaping them as they chose, leaving a small box of white space here and there to tell the essence of the story in words---in 647 characters thank you, including punctuation and spaces between words.

And from Peter there we learned that this smokejumper story was to be only about one-fourth of a larger photo-essay, 12 to 14 pages, that he was shooting of the entire U.S. Forest Service, he having gone around to four or five interesting, diverse locations in the National Forests across the whole nation to get his pix.

But fire and fate wiped out Peter's 12-page Forest Service spread in LIFE---and all that work---just as they later wiped out his beautiful home in the hills above Oakland, California in 1991, along with a lifetime of a photographer's files and cameras and pictures and mementos. For on August 5, 1949, twelve young smokejumpers (plus one young fireguard who had been a smokejumper the year before) were trapped by a firestorm in Mann Gulch of the Helena National Forest, Montana, and burned to death. Three other jumpers on that fire---Wag Dodge, the foreman, and Walt Rumsey and Bob Sallee, parachute-firemen---survived. Of course the disaster made news around the world---the shock of which caused the LIFE editors to kill the original Forest Service spread in favor of using only the photos that could illustrate the disaster story--- including ones that Peter Stackpole could get by a quick return flight to the scene of the tragedy. And that is what you saw in the August 22 issue of LIFE that year, a five-page spread on the Mann Gulch disaster, with a dozen of the victims shown in full life before the firestorm, and the three survivors after.

        After the funerals and the weeping and the fire season were over, back at home in New Mexico I found in my own color slides a good shot of Peter Stackpole, two or three cameras hanging on his stomach, as he chatted with a few of the red-hatted smokejumpers at rest. Knowing that working photographers seldom get a shot of themselves at work, I sent it to him. In the note that went with it I asked him only that if he ever found a good smokejumper photo he could spare, I would appreciate seeing it. For a long time nothing happened. Then months later a large packet arrived marked PHOTOS; PLEASE DO NOT CRUSH---from Peter Stackpole of LIFE. Inside were four (count 'em) 11 x 14 outstanding LIFE smokejumper pictures---Ford Trimotors, DC-3's, men and equipment displays, and jumpers leaping from the plane---with Peter's captions penciled on the backs. And lo and behold, unbeknownst to Peter, I was even in one of them.

It was these great photos that I wanted to show to Peter and his friends on this their reunion to honor Mark Kauffman at Cal Poly.

When the show was over, and everyone had visited the exhibit hall, and the vintage LIFE photographers finished posing for group shots to celebrate their reunion, the moment had come. I barged into the group, asking if anyone would like to see some original LIFE photos by Peter Stackpole in his prime. Naturally they all did. And the editors enjoyed it too, panning Peter of course for writing lousy captions on the backs.

So a week later I wrote Peter, up at his new home in Novato, suggesting that, when he'd finished his current book on Hollywood, he consider bringing out this book, making use of the best of all those fine LIFE photos that never made it into LIFE, and do this solely as his next Stackpole photo book. And I said if he decided to do such a thing, he could use my Saturday Evening Post article, "We Jump Into Fire," and the Bob Sallee Mann Gulch Memorial talk at no charge. (Bob Sallee had previously given me permission to try to get that excellent talk published.)

Well, Peter wrote back that he wanted to do the book---but he wanted me to be co-author with him, with me doing all the writing and him being in charge of all the photography. Now I ask you, what smokejumper writer could pass up an offer like that from Peter Stackpole?

So here it is. <u>Smokejumpers, '49: Brothers in the Sky</u>.

Thanks, Mark Kauffman.

PROLOG

In 1940 the U.S. Forest Service pioneered a new concept in fighting forest fires in the wilderness timber of the Northwest: Flying firefighters in quickly by plane and dropping them by parachute near the fire so they could hit it fast while it was still small. They started calling such airborne firefighters smokejumpers---and for more than 54 years the name has not only stuck but become venerated.

The first crude techniques of this art were worked out near Winthrop, Washington on the Chelan National Forest after the fire season of 1939. There test jumpers, some from the parachute company furnishing the chutes, made 58 experimental leaps to learn how to drop men into the timber without getting them skewered by snags or pine trees.

The next year young Forest Service men Earl Cooley and Rufus Robinson of Missoula made the first fire jump July 12, 1940 near Moose Creek, Idaho. Earl's chute streamered for most of the way down and the spotter nearly fell out of the

plane; but both jumpers landed intact and fought
the little lightning-strike and put it out. They were
soon followed by Francis Lufkin and Glenn Smith
who jumped on another fire August 10 near
Winthrop, Washington in the North Cascades, the
first fire jump in Region Six of the Forest Service.

Since war was looming, the U.S. Army sent
officers to see how this was done in order to
develop the concept for the Army paratroopers.
They got some good lessons, some of which they
put to use in the war.

Back in the woods the fire seasons of '41
and '42 saw expanded use of smokejumpers with
a 26-man crew operating out of Missoula. During
the rest of World War II, since most able-bodied
young men were in the military, the infant
smokejumper program was carried on by the
despised conscientious objectors serving as
parachute-firemen for no pay except room and
board. They did all that to prove that, though
opposed to killing in warfare, they were not
cowards. And they saved the smokejumpers from
extinction.

After the war the CO's lost their
smokejumper jobs and were replaced by returning
veterans, with preference generally given to GI Bill
college students majoring in forestry. But all
jumper candidates had to be experienced firefighters first and then be eager to work hard and
undergo parachute training.

Soon the smokejumper base at Missoula
was expanded to 150 jumpers, and other bases
were developed at McCall, Idaho (50 men);
Winthrop, Washington (about 30); and Cave

Junction, Oregon (also 30). There was also a temporary base set up every spring in Silver City, New Mexico (about 30 men). This one was made up of migrating northern jumpers who flew down with their equipment to protect the giant Gila National Forest during the earlier Southwest fire season of May through July 4th.

Though smokejumping remained essentially a 3-month summer job for loggers between jobs, college students and teachers, a few of its pioneers and leaders worked year-round for the Forest Service developing equipment and making the huge necessary preparations for each far-flung summer.

Eventually California established a base near Redding to cover northern California national forests; and the Cave Junction, Oregon base was moved to the airport near Redmond to better serve that whole state. Also the Bureau of Land Management developed smokejumper bases out of Boise, Idaho and in Alaska, using the more modern, softer-landing parachutes adopted by the McCall, Idaho base.

Though many other airborne techniques followed smokejumping---the use of helicopters and "helitack" crews, fire-retardant-dropping tankers, fireboss scouting planes, aerial fire patrols---because of their economy, smokejumpers continue to be a mainstay of western back-country fire control. Today there are about 400 smoke-jumpers from New Mexico to Alaska, a small number compared to the totals of ground-based fire crews fielded in the dozen forested western states. And each one of them is proud to be a member of this most elite corps of firefighters.

My two summers in jumping were in 1948 out of Cave Junction and 1949 out of Missoula. My younger brother Hugh was a smokejumper with me in '49 and this collection is twenty-one stories from that experience. Hugh went back to Missoula the summers of 1950 and '51. During those last 2 seasons, one cool and wet and one hot and dry, he also participated in the making of the Hollywood film, RED SKIES OF MONTANA, starring Richard Widmark and Jeffrey Hunter. At one point for the movie Hugh Jenkins leaped out in a mass jump of 24 men coming out of a DC-3 and a Ford Trimotor flying in formation---an unheard of procedure on any actual fire jump.

The dangers of the job are plentiful, as we found out with a vengeance in August with the Mann Gulch disaster, and as four other jumpers rediscovered in the similar Glenwood Springs, Colorado disaster of July 6, 1994. Yet the attractions of the job are such that many jumpers get addicted to the adrenalin high, coming back year after year, wishing to remain forever among that elite fraternity, the brothers in the sky.

We Jump Into Fire

I'm up in the hot sun cutting a tin valley
drain for the new loft roof we're putting on when
the call comes in. "Eight men on Yellowstone
Park! One plane load. Cole, Jenkins, Samsel, Hall,
Hellman, Bennett, Piper, Thol! Get your gear and
let's go. Fire Jump!"

It is 1:40 on a summer afternoon. The
Forest Service Parachute Loft, at Missoula,
Montana, is having a busy week. Fires are
popping all over the region, and planes are
shuttling men out to jump and back home to rest
as long as daylight will let them. We're running
out of jump rations and have to order truckloads of
C rations from War Surplus, and the riggers are
working overtime to get the chutes packed as
those big white bundles of loose nylon come in.
One fabulous Thursday within the last few weeks,
sixty-four men jumped on fires scattered over the
wild 25,000,000 acres that is the Forest Service's
Region One. And a week later thirty-four men
were dropped in twos and fours and sometimes
dozens from the Gallatin Forest, down near
Wyoming, to the Kaniksu, up in Washington State.

"All right you guys, Shank will be spotting you, and you'll land at West Yellowstone to pick up the park man. He'll have maps for you and give you your best routes out. Now get that gear into the plane."

We've been loading a pickup with half a ton of equipment: Back-pack chutes in white canvas covers; chest-pack reserves, compact and olive drab with red rip rings; big bulky sacks that contain our canvas jump suits, helmets, letdown ropes and harnesses. Fire packs with rations, canteens, flashlights, fire tools---a shovel and a pulaski, and a file for sharpening them---all wrapped tightly in new tarps and mounted on clack-board carriers for the hike out. Sleeping bags---big kapok ones this time instead of the tiny, efficient goose-down rolls we sometimes have along on fires. Five-gallon water cans---silvery square oblongs of steel that we know from experience smash as often as not on landing---tied in pairs to cargo chutes. Then lots of odds and ends, like a spotter's kit, map cases with compasses, climbing irons for retrieving chutes, extra signal streamers and a crosscut saw bolted between two boards, so that its sharp-set teeth won't be ruined on landing.

Outside, the plane is a sight to frighten the wits out of a modern air passenger. It is an ancient tri-motor job, its engines uncowled, with external control cables that slap its corrugated aluminum sides in the wind, truck tires on huge solid wheels, large square windows like a streetcar and the over-all streamlining of a Model T. The wing is massive and fat, and the fuselage seems

cut off square at the bottom to clear the turf of the
airport. The wing-mounted engines have three
dials each on the inboard side of one strut, so that
the pilot, to check the engine's performance, must
look through rain, darkness or fog and find those
dials. This museum piece of an aircraft has been
known variously as The Heap, The Tin Goose, The
Flying Quonset Hut and Old Ironsides.

Yet we who are about to fly in her feel good
inside, knowing that she is light for her size and
can get in and out of canyons and postage-stamp
airstrips. We know that the pudgy three-foot-thick
wing gives her tremendous lift---she can glide and
glide if the engines fail. We know that the high
wing and big square windows give us visibility,
and visibility is important in this business of
jumping on fires. We know also that she, like her
sister ships, has been kept up by her owner---
Johnson Flying Service, aerial contractor to the
Forest Service in Region 1---to the best of man's
ability.

Now the pickup roars out to where the plane
is thundering in warm-up, and we transfer the load
into her belly and climb in ourselves. Take-off-
time, two o'clock. We are scrambling around in
the great jumble of equipment as the airport and
the fairgrounds and Missoula drop away below.
We swing past the big white M of the University of
Montana on the side of Sentinel Mountain and then
settle on a southeast course bound for Yellowstone country.

Two hundred miles from Missoula to West
Yellowstone. A two-hour flight in the slow-moving
plane. We climb to clear the ridges that bristle up

before us, and there always seem to be higher ones beyond. Getting cool as we climb. The door of the plane is off and back in Missoula, and a safety bar stretches across the middle of the doorway to keep guys from falling out.

Smitty, the chief rigger, is along for the ride ---the same Glenn Smith who made the first fire jump in Region 6 in August of 1940. He is telling us not to hit the ground in high country like Yellowstone or we'll break our ankles like he did on his last jump up there in '47.

"Small reproduction, young trees---that's what you want to look for. Small reproduction for a soft landing. But hang up, whatever you do." Then Smitty goes up forward to gab with the pilot and fly the old Goose awhile, horsing it sloppily over the next pass till the pilot takes the controls away from him and adds a little throttle for good measure.

"Hey, that must be Georgetown Lake!"

"Yeah, there's Anaconda over there. See the big smelters?" Eleven thousand feet to clear the highest range. It's cold up here in the air-conditioned plane. Seems funny; an hour ago I was sweating, out on that roof in Missoula's heat. Now I'm shaking with cold and pawing through the big white sacks to find mine and break out my high-collared canvas jump jacket.

Big stone mountains with jagged tops go by. I'd hate to jump into stuff like that. Don't worry, you won't have to. The Forest Service isn't out of its head.

The ranges are getting drier, less timbered, more and more just big humpy ridges of bareness

separating the twisting river valleys with their
bright-green irrigated fields. We're slanting down
over Hebgen Reservoir, and my ears are popping in
a glide. Must be close to West Yellowstone. We
start suiting up---too early, but everybody starts,
so I do too. Dumping our sacks out on the
crowded floor of the plane, fighting our way into
our girdles and jackets and jump pants with the big
webbing crotch protection, and our quick-release
harnesses.

"You can put on the chutes later, guys, after
we pick up the park man." So we don't fasten
our legstraps, but sit comfortably half dressed for a
jump, and I'm taking pictures with the 35-mm.
camera that I take on all fires these days.

"Hey, there's West Yellowstone!"

We give the town a good buzz with two
steeply banked circles to lose altitude, and West
Yellowstone, with its railroad station and lodge and
airstrip and stores, and two highways slicing away
through the endless plateau of timber, is wheeling
below us like a big, slow pinwheel. Then the pilot
is down where he wants to be, and we skitter in
over the clawing lodgepole to a landing on the dirt
strip.

We taxi over for gas and to find the park
man, and all pile out for a stretch. Hot again down
here. Why did we suit up so soon? Smitty and
Hank Shank are out hunting for the park man while
we sprawl in the shade of the plane's protective
wing. Soon they are back in a black Park Service
car, and they pile out with two National Park
rangers. These are dressed in snappy green-and-
gray uniforms that we in the Forest Service think

make them look just a little too much like tourist
ushers. But forget the rivalry. We're working
together this time. Besides, the Park Service pays
for maintaining ten of our 150 jumpers at
Missoula, so that the park people can call on the
outfit for fire protection whenever Glacier or
Yellowstone needs it.

"One of the fires has a ground crew on it
already," Shank is saying. So Hellman and Bennett
unsuit to stay here at West Yellowstone. Hellman
fits his harness and reserve onto the ranger that's
going to guide the remaining six of us to our three
remote spot fires. Shank is reshuffling the jump
list, and I want to jump last, so I can take pictures
of the guys going out the door. But I don't say
anything, and he puts me in the first pair---with
Kermit Cole, of Missoula, a good boy.

Cole and I didn't find out till Saturday
afternoon that the last four men of our eight-man
load---Hellman, Bennett, Thol and Piper---all made
dry runs on Yellowstone and went back to
Missoula to jump on Friday and die in Helena
National Forest. And I wanted to go last to take
pictures!

We suit up again, this time chutes and all,
and check one another out. Harnesses secure all
around; safety catches of our quick-releases on;
three little strings under the loop of each static line
to secure the apex of the chute to its cover till our
weight tears it loose. A dozen little details that
have to be right. Our right legs look fat with a
100 foot coil of rope stuffed in the leg pocket.
And my left leg is also bulging with a small
strapped-on canvas sack of personal gear---soap,

toothbrush, clean socks, underwear and
dungarees. We'll be almost unrecognizable when
we get our football helmets on with the wire grill
face masks buckled down. Six hundred dollars
worth of equipment. Seventy pounds of fabric and
rope and metal per man, not counting the stuff
that goes in by cargo chute.

The engines are thundering again, and the
park man yells to the pilot, "Got plenty of gas?
We've gotta fly fifty miles one direction, then
seventy miles another, then forty miles back."

"Yeah, we've got plenty."

All aboard again except Hellman and
Bennett---the last I ever see of them alive---and
we're roaring down the runway in take-off. The
park man has an armful of map scrolls, and he's
having a tough time climbing forward over the
jumble of men and equipment in the seatless
tunnel-like plane. He's brought a feeble little water
bag along to drop to one of his ground crews. A
two-gallon job with about half a gallon in it---and
that leaking out through the loose cap as the bag
lies on its side by the door, jiggling with the plane
vibration. Hate to be out on a mountain and have
to depend on that. Our smashable square water
cans don't look half bad alongside this park brand
of water supply.

The ranger is a nice guy, and he's done this
before. As soon as he knows that Cole and I are
on the first stick, he gives me a little piece of a
Yellowstone topographic map with some lakes and
a couple of rivers on it and an inked-in X and some
arrows running west and north from the X. The X
is the fire, of course---as close as they can tell

from the Mount Sheridan lookout, and incidentally about a half mile off, as we find out later---and the little river nearby is the headwaters of the Snake. The thick green line right below the X is the southern border of the park---less than three miles from the fire. So that'll put us 250 miles straight southeast of Missoula. The ranger is explaining that the arrows point the way out.

"Don't go back this way on the trail," he shouts above the roaring engines, "even though it looks closer, because that trail hasn't been maintained! Go north, the way it's marked, to the ranger station on Heart Lake!"

"Roger," I say, and put the map away and start taking pictures again. It's great being a second-year jumper and having a little experience to give you confidence. It's more fun knowing the little tricks that take your mind off yourself--- enough to keep from sweating like Samsel, or Piper, there. Short Hall seems kinda quiet too. Oh, well, last year you sweated just like they're doing.

We're over the valley of the Snake, and the Grand Tetons rear their heads in jagged black majesty forty miles to the south. Hank Shank, our handsome spotter, is motioning me back to where Cole is sitting by the door, waiting. The ranger is up with Smitty and the pilot, looking for the smoke, and I take a last snapshot of Cole before tucking my camera inside my jacket and under my arm, where it hasn't smashed yet on a landing.

"There it is!" I say, poking Hank Shank and pointing to a smoke off the port quarter. The smoke isn't much, and Cole and I figure we really

are going on a one-man fire, but two of us along
for safety. Word is passed to the pilot, and we get
down to business. Cole and I put on our gloves
and helmets and snap our collars all the way up
and get our static lines over our arms and into our
right hands.

There's a wilderness of snags below us---
miles and miles of dead-white tree skeletons
marching over the hills as far as we can see
individual trees. The old Heart Lake burn, the
ranger said, in 1931, and still looking ugly after all
those years.

Snags. One of the four dangerous horsemen
facing the smokejumper; the others being deep
water, sheer rock and insecure tree hang-ups.
Cole and Hank Shank and Smitty and I are all
looking for a decent place to land in that tossing
ocean of brittle dead bones; and we all
simultaneously decide on the only spot available---
a stand of thick young reproduction about a mile
along the ridge from the smoke. I've got the map
out again, getting oriented with the terrain, and
100 per cent of my attention is on the problem of
getting to the ground safely. Ground altitude
almost 8000 feet here. "Remember, hang up,
whatever you do!" A little drift chute gives Hank
the wind---something like twelve miles an hour,
blowing east---and then comes the order to hook
up.

Cole and I snap our static lines into the
cable over the door and give ourselves a last fast
check-out. Cole is going out first, so he kneels in
the oval door and puts one foot out on the little
step hanging there in space. I'm going out

second, so I crouch behind him ready to follow him out as soon as the door is clear. Shank checks us over carefully again and briefs us once more on the spot we're to aim for and repeats what the ranger said about hiking out. Then we swing into the final pass, Shank jockeying the plane into position with hand signals to the pilot. The noisy engines die at last, and after one second of eerie silence, Cole gets the slap to go. He steps out easy and straight, wrapping his arms across the reserve on his chest, and the static line begins reeling the white silk off his back. I'm out with him a half second later, feeling the weird minutes-long moment of falling before the opening shock jolts me in the chest, and then that wonderful nylon flower is open above me with the sunlight streaming through.

No lines over---canopy functioning perfectly. Cole is far enough away. Okay, where is that spot? There it is, the lightest green of that patch of timber. Turn away from it and hold into the wind. I grab a guideline to spin myself west---for this is a steerable, slotted Forest Service chute I'm wearing---and haul down the front risers to gain forward speed.

I'm chinning myself on the risers to give myself eight or maybe ten miles an hour into the wind. The plane is circling around watching us closely and is completely out of my consciousness. Damned arms are getting tired, and I'm watching the ground through the V of my feet. I'm not going to make it; the wind's pushing me too far. And yet for some reason I'm not worried at all that I'm sailing beyond the thick safe stand of young trees toward the open, tree-dotted ridge.

Gettin' pretty close. Better stop planing and turn around. The slots start me around so I'll come in frontward, and I'm not quite around, and dumping both slots to kill forward speed, when the grassy ground with all the trees just out of reach rushes up into me with a thump. My feet are together from habit, and I flop into a loose sideways roll and come up tangled, unhurt and happy.

A soft landing, considering the 8000 feet. No harder than plenty of jumps I've made at 2000 or 3000. Well, that just shows what queer ducks parachutes are. The air must be perfect today.

Cole has also hit the ground 100 yards away from me and behind a couple of trees. We are both waving our signal streamers at the plane to show them we're all right, and then we're climbing out of our gear and sacking it up. The plane goes away to drop Samsel and Short on a smoke we can't see, beyond the Snake, and comes back ten minutes later to drop our cargo. We have piled our sacked-up gear in an orange-streamered cache on the ridge and watch our cargo come out of the plane a mile away through the forest of snags. The watercan chute hangs up in the top of a big snag right near the vague haze of smoke, and the silvery tin twirls and twinkles in the sun, making a perfect landmark for us to hike for.

Okay, Jenkins, the fun is over. Now begins the work you're getting paid for. The noise of the plane tapers away to nothing, and all of a sudden it's quiet on this mountain. Cole and I are two guys alone in the wilderness. Alone, many miles from the nearest road, in a sunny, dead forest.

"Damn Smitty for forgetting to drop the sleeping bags!"

"Oh, well," says Cole, full of good sense, as always, "That just means we'll work most of the night. And those kapoks are plenty big to pack out."

He's right, and I know it, and I don't mind working most of the night anyway to rake in a little overtime.

The fire is up on a knoll the way most lightning strikes are, and isn't going anywhere since the wind died down. It's really a tiny fire---at the size the Forest Service likes to catch them--- not covering 100 square feet---in five or six little spots, where the lightning split off chunks of a snag and scattered them, burning, out on the grass. The stump of the snag is twenty feet high and burning all the way up and down inside, and dropping it will be our biggest single job in putting out this fire.

We're a little short on water because when we felled the snag that held our watercan way up in the air, the can smashed to tinfoil and the water wetted up the ground good. Besides that, one of the canteens on the firepacks had a leak and is dry, so we have half a gallon from the other canteen to last us till we hike down to the Snake tomorrow sometime. Not that we'll need any more than that half gallon. But knowing that's all we've got is making us thirsty already.

It's been a big job falling a snag three feet through at the butt with a pulaski just to get down the cargo chute---a pulaski being a heavy-headed axe with an adz blade on the back. Cole and I have taken turns and are really warmed up by the time she sways and cracks and comes crashing down among the jumble of deadfalls around us.

We collect the gear and eat supper, hitting the liquid canned stuff first to save our water, and then settle down for a night of work. The tall butt of the burning snag comes down first and doubles the spread of the fire by taking an unexpected roll. We cool the burning logs by turning them warm side up and scraping the fire out of them with the adz blades of the pulaskis. We break the big embers up into little ones and spread out the hot spots to cool and burn out. Then we trail each little spot of burn, scraping a shallow shovel-width trench around it down to fireproof mineral earth.

"Separate the fuel from the fire"---the old simplicity-itself firefighting method of the Forest Service. It doesn't take water or chemicals or bombs or pumps or hoses, though all those things may help if available. All it takes in essence is men, enough men with tools, and lots of sweat and backbending and shiny places on the insides of thumbs. And half-decent luck in regard to wind. But like any firefighting method, it works best at night, when everything cools down.

It's midnight and cold, and the stars are so bright you can almost see by 'em, and the northern lights are a faint gray glow in the sky that looks like dawn coming up in the wrong place. Cole and I are sitting around patrolling our little line and taking turns going up to a muddy sump of a spring we found to fill two water bags with the stagnant stuff and pour it on what spots are still glowing red in the darkness. There's not much smoke drifting up through the cones of light from our head-lamp flashlights any more. The night is still and without wind. And the fire is just about dead.

So we decide to stretch out for a couple of hours, wrapping up in the tarps from the firepacks and the cargo chutes to keep warm. Not as cold as I'd expected it to be, and two hours of good shut-eye really pick me up. <u>Don't forget to put that on the time report, that we slept for two hours</u>.

Up again at two for a long cold morning of mop-up. We douse every square foot of the burn with undrinkable water and go over the charred ground with our gloves off, feeling for warm spots. It seems I'm spending half the night slogging back and forth to the shallow sump, filling the water bags tediously with a skillet, and climbing endlessly over the tangled maze of fallen snags back to the fire.

It's dawn and beautiful, and there's Mount Sheridan to the north and the valley of the Snake below us, and we're filthy and tired and unshaven, and the fire is dead. We eat breakfast, griping again because there's too much chocolate and ham in these jump rations, and the last of our canned fruit and juice goes, and all but a couple of swallows of water. Oh, well, there's a whole river of it right down there. We'll make out all right.

We know we'll have to watch the burn through at least two o'clock this afternoon to make sure that somewhere in that black wet mess of charcoal we haven't missed one spark, because

the heat of the afternoon will show smoke if
there's going to be any. So we figure we'll use
this half day to start packing out. Chutes, suits,
firepacks and tools will make a good muleload for
each of us. And as we have time to burn, we
might as well make two trips.

It's a mile back along the ridge to our jump
gear, and then three miles down to the river trail---
all through the maddening tangle of downed snags
that blankets this country. About 80 per cent of
the deadfalls lie with their tops to the east, telling
us mutely that the winds roar through this saddle
from the west most of the time. We pack down
our jump gear---two big, heavy white sacks apiece
lashed to a clackboard---and it's treacherous
footing downhill over the never-ending snags. Five
or six elk are moving down ahead of us, keeping a
good half mile away and wondering what men are
doing prowling around their domain. It's marshy
grassland in the bottoms, with fresh elk wallows
and lots of flies, and a flock of black-headed
Canada geese takes off ahonking from the Snake
as we trudge into sight.

A soft little rain starts to fall, and we know
the fire is out for good---even though we'll check it
again to make sure when we go back after the
rations and fire tools. We get squared away with
our map, discovering the half-mile error in the
original fire location from the layout of the trail
with the river; and it's good to have a full canteen
again.

Six o'clock, Thursday evening. The sunlight
is bright and warm, and I've just taken a bath in a
creek because the mighty Snake here is too

shallow to get underwater in. Cole is busy eating
supper---something I shall later regret not doing---
and we've found, from horse tracks and shouting
up and down the valley, what the dope is on the
packer who is to lug this load the rest of the way
out on packsaddles. The packer has been up here
looking for us and has gone beyond where we
have come out on the trail. So we quit looking for
him, pile everything beside the trail, barber-pole a
tree with streamers, so he can't miss, and start
hiking for the ranger station up on Heart Lake.

     Our map shows it to be six miles away.
With all the twists and turns of the trail it turns out
to be twelve. My boots are stretched and too big,
and there's a place on my heel that makes a little
squeaking sound with every step as it rubs on the
inside of the boot.

     Pretty soon it's dark and we wonder if we
are on the right trail, and the moon comes up in
time to help out Cole's waning flashlight. On a
needlessly empty stomach and with one bad foot, I
am a poor partner for a strong hiker like Cole, and
he is constantly having to stop and wait for me.
Another herd of elk is moving ahead of us in the
darkness, crashing away intermittently when the
tortured bawling of their scouts warns them of our
persistent approach. The black peak of Mount
Sheridan seems an eternity in creeping down to
our left, and then at midnight we are finally
marching along the shore of Heart Lake, feeling
triumphantly near to rest. Suddenly we get a jolt,
for there, a few hundred yards away, is a tall
plume of smoke climbing into the moonlit sky.
Another fire. But the fear quickly evaporates as a

stink of sulphur drifts over us. <u>A hot spring</u>. <u>That
isn't smoke; that's steam</u>. <u>You're still in
Yellowstone, remember</u>?

The ranger station is nothing more than
what the Forest Service calls a guard station---just
a cabin that may or may not be manned during the
summer, the fire season. This one is manned by
the packer who is out looking for us, and is well
stocked with provisions. It looks beautiful there in
the moonlight on the sandy north shore of the
lake, and we find the break-in window in the back
with no strain. The lake is so clean and remote
from people that a bucket dipped out of it is
drinking water---a weird contrast to the highway
cluttered with people and monoxide fumes just
across the mountains.

A quick chow to stifle my gnawing gut, and
the blankets close over us in sleep . . .

"Hey, Kerm, did you shave back there in the
cabin?" Cole is hiking ahead of me on the trail out
from Heart Lake to the roadhead, and I can't see
his face from where I'm walking. "Hell, no! I
wouldn't shave in cold water for all of Yellowstone
National Park."

As if smarting under the insult, Yellowstone
National Park produces, 100 yards farther up the
trail, plenty of hot running water for all our needs.
We squat on a steaming lime flat among countless
bubbling hot springs for our first shave in three
days. The water is too hot to be used for anything
except dipping a washrag, but we make out. And
we find the creek nearby has all degrees of
mixtures from boiling to cold, as the surface water
mixes with that from underground.

I get a scare a little later when I slip
shin-deep into some warm volcanic muck while
crossing another open flat. It's not pleasant
thinking of the people who have died of accidental
scalding in Yellowstone's strange, naturally hot
waters. But the mud goes to my boot tops and no
farther, and I churn loose like a shying horse. The
mud on my boots dries to white crust as we hike
on out.

A truck meets us at the road five miles
farther on, and after we make our fire report at the
South Gate, the Park Service sends us on a
personally-conducted tour of the park, the first leg
of our long ground trip home. We're stuck in
Mammoth Village, on the north edge of the park,
that evening because we can't get a train out of
Livingston, Montana, till morning; and we kill time
at a dance and a touristy wildlife lecture. Cole and
I sit in the back row and grin when the ranger tells
how nine forest fires are going in the park right
now, and how they've called in extra crews and
planes and even smokejumpers.

All next day we ride the train back to
Missoula and gripe because it's Saturday and
we're traveling on our own time. But then, in the
station at Missoula, we pick up a red-headlined
paper that tells us twelve of our buddies were
burned to death yesterday afternoon down in the
Helena. It's hard to believe that Dave Navon, my
best friend in this outfit, won't ever be back to get
that laughing postcard I sent him from Old Faithful.
And Cole and I are shocked and hollow and hungry
to know why, and we feel powerful lucky to have
gone on our Yellowstone jump.

Redwood Mountain Diary
(of Hugh J. Jenkins)

Saturday, June 21, 1947
Redwood Mountain BRC Camp
Sequoia National Park, California

Last Tuesday all of us new boys went over
to Red Fir for instruction in fighting forest fires.
The rangers gave us good training. They taught us
to wear hats with brims and turn down the brims
to keep sparks from singeing our heads. And how
to wear long-sleeved work shirts and leave the
shirt-tails out---to let the sparks and twigs that did
go down your neck shake on through. We learned
the first rule of safety in fireline building is to keep
ten feet apart so that no man chops or spades his
buddy by mistake. And a corollary to this is that
when you're walking through thick brush or low
tree limbs---TEN FEET APART---you don't hold the
branch out of the way of your buddy (because that
means you're getting too close together again) but
you just push on through it and let it swing back---
and if he gets hit in the face it means he's

following too close.

The rangers taught us something about the different tools, such as a mcleod---also called a kortik---(a square blade at right angles to its handle, which has a rake on one-side and a flat cutting edge on the other), a pulaski (a heavy axe with a little hoe on the back side of the blade), a brush hook (a big knife for cutting brush), and above all the plain axe and the plain round-bladed shovel. A few men are also trained in using the six-foot crosscut saw.

We learned how to use a mcleod and a shovel to scrape away the duff (the burnable layer of old needles, twigs, grass and leaves) down to good mineral earth (fireproof stuff). And most important we learned how to throw a shovel-full of dirt twenty feet into a hotspot to cool it down. A few guys were made axe men to head the fireline and a few pairs were trained to pull the crosscut saw to slice sections of log out of deadfalls and to also sometimes drop burning snags (dead trees). And we all got snakebite training and snakebite kits to be ready for rattlers---something we need every day in Blister Rust Control work in this Sierra country. (Lots of timber rattlers in these parts.)

The main thing in firefighting is to build, or clear, a fireline around the burning area. A line of men is formed, the front men carrying axes and brush hooks, the next few men alternating between shovels, kortiks (mcleods) and pulaskis. The last pair of men or sometimes the 2nd or 3rd pair, will have a crosscut saw about six feet long, but one man will carry it bowed in a loop with a sliced piece of fire-hose tied over its sharp teeth to

keep from getting cut on it. The other man usually
carries a large 2-gallon canteen and they trade off.
And they also carry an oil can to lubricate the
blade when it gets sticky with pitch, and wedges
and a hammer to wedge open the cut when the log
starts to pinch the blade. And of course each man
needs good boots, sturdy work clothes and strong
leather work gloves. The line of men moves along
around the burning area, each man taking a few
swipes at chopping or scraping a path down to
unburnable mineral soil. You don't worry about
getting it perfect but keep on taking swipes at it
and moving along. By the time twenty men have
gone by there's a pretty good barrier there, and
when you come around it again (if it's a small fire--
-say less than a couple of acres) you then can
widen and deepen the line, cut out roots and
branches that might carry the fire across, and put
certain men on special danger points, like dropping
a burning snag or checking for spot fires over the
line, etc.

        In the afternoon we built a practice line up
the mountainside. And we found out why firefighters get lots of blisters and aching backs and
why they have to be in good shape and be really
willing to work hard.

        The instruction was just in time. That night
at 12:30 the lights went on and we were rolled
out to go on a fire. I climbed into my new levis,
my best blue shirt and my work shoes, stuffed an
extra pair of socks in my pocket, and climbed into
the open back of the stakeside truck with
everybody else. It was a long, cold ride. The
truck twisted up the dirt track leading to the main

highway and then roared down toward the foothills. As we sped around the curves the headlights raked across the woods. After an hour or so the truck left the timber and the road was bordered by the scrubby stuff of the lower country. We all sat huddled in the truck, either hidden under a blanket or shivering in the wind.

The ride lasted for a long time. At 4:30 Wednesday morning we pulled up at the fire camp which had already been set up, ate a good breakfast, and started to work about six. Each of us carried a heavy gallon canteen in addition to our little quarts. We lined up for tools, and I was handed a pulaski. On the way up the mountain we met the regular Forest Service boys who had been working since six the night before. They looked pretty weary. The fire covered two slopes of a small mountain, about 160 acres, which is fairly big. The FS boys had completed the heavy work, and the fire was out except for an occasional blazing tree or log. The fireline had been cleared, and it was our job to mop up.

We started out in single file to go up the mountain. It was a stinking climb. At first we followed the creek bed, walking unevenly over the rocks. Then we turned off to go up a minor water course, and the sweat started to roll. If we weren't wriggling up over slippery charred grass we were clambering up over slide rock, kicking down small boulders for those below to dodge. The slope was in many places at a 60 percent angle. I sweated more than I ever have before.

We separated into crews and started mopping up. From eight till noon we moved over the burnt area, chopping, raking and digging. From noon till 6 PM the job was easy; we simply "patrolled," which meant sitting under a tree and glancing around occasionally to guard against flare-ups.

At six we went down, filthy as apes and thirsty as sailors. We had another good meal, which included some heavenly milk. After supper we went down to Kings River, which rushed by near the camp, and washed up. My shirt looked as if I'd been wearing it three weeks. My new levis had dyed my shorts blue. My socks had more dirt than fabric in them. I had a good bath, though; and we dried ourselves by sitting on the warm rocks as the sun went down.

Each of us drew two blankets and slept on the ground. We were roused at 4:30 AM and worked from six to six again doing the same work. I carried a shovel on Thursday. Another fellow and I got off by ourselves. His watch was wrong and we didn't know it. We ate lunch at about three o'clock, thinking it was noon. We had gotten damn hungry and the morning had seemed to last forever. The crewleader told us to go in at quarter to five, and at what we thought was 2:30 a fellow came by and told us it was 5:30. It was a big surprise. We hurried back to camp, ate, got credit for thirty-three hours of work (including six hours of travel time), and climbed back into the truck. At $1.05 an hour we earned quite a bit of money. We were back at Redwood Mountain by 10 PM Thursday.

Wednesday, August 13, 1947

Big brother Starr just wrote telling how he followed my suggestion and got on for blister-rust work too this summer. He even thanked me for suggesting it. He's up in the Stanislaus National Forest north of Yosemite in a place called Camp Bumblebee with 44 other men. They're off the Sonora Pass Road near a town called Strawberry. Pinecrest Lake, with lots of summer homes and pretty girls and sailboats, is just four miles by trail over the mountain, or seven miles around by road. Out in the sugar pine woods at 6500 feet they have lots of rattlers, but they've also had four fires so far to liven up the ribeys eradication. One was down in the Gold Rush country of Calaveras County, and it was l0,000 acres. Starr always has been a lucky cuss.

Last Tuesday the much-yearned-for and long awaited fire call came to Redwood Mountain. A group of us down at the Wilsonia Lodge had to leave our delicious banana splits unconsumed and hop on the truck heading back to camp. Roy, who was driving, brought the truck to a sweeping halt in the parking area, and we piled noisily off to run into the barracks and get our fire clothes on.

We found out it was just a standby call; and after the initial excitement wore off, a reaction set in. I marked it off mentally as another false alarm, took off my canteen, put away my gloves, hat and jacket, and picked up a book. But a few minutes after chow Jeff honked the horn and told us to get ready. We climbed into the trucks, and at 6 PM they rolled us away toward Giant Forest.

The fire was in the Kaweah River Canyon,

some miles east of Giant Forest. The two trucks
whirled over the neat little roads leading through
that beautiful forest of sequoias, swept around the
village, and pulled into the Kaweah firecamp by
about eight. The country around Giant Forest is
lovely as can be: no brush, simply one great tree
after another shutting out the sky and making a
vast, cool dusky quiet room.

At about nine we were issued headlamps
and tools, and we started in one long line toward
the fire. We were on the west ridge above the
Kaweah, the fire smoking softly and steadily in the
canyon below us, and we could see the high,
jagged east ridge, lying blue and strong straight
across from us. The ridge was interesting, as all
ridges are, for what it hid from us; the great Kern
River Canyon, and farther yet, the High Sierras
near Mount Whitney.

We followed our ridge awhile, trying to find
a way down. Finally Murdock, the ranger who
was leading us, simply picked a fairly promising
gully and we started down, a long, twisting sliding
line of lights. It was a tricky slide. (Murdock said
later he'd never have tried it in the daytime when
he could see what he was heading into). The
brush wasn't impossible, but we ran into some
fields of slick rock which made rather difficult
crossings. Yet everybody got down all right.

Every few minutes Murdock would holler
back "Break!" and everyone would squat down,
the line of lights would flicker out, and we'd sit in
the stillness looking down at the flame below. It
was a fairly brilliant, even spectacular sight---an
area about half-a-mile square, dotted with little

torches and splashed with big lines of fire.
Occasionally a sudden flare-up would mark where
a good-sized tree had gone up in flames in a few
seconds.

We moved around under one line of flames
and started building a fire trail, Roy's crew moving
south and Bill's crew going north. The fire was
burning right down toward us, but we managed to
stop it, to my surprise. Several times I had to
scoop up coals which had rolled down into the
fireline and heave them back up into the burning
side. I had a shovel, and since we were short of
shovels, I had a busy time ducking back and forth
through the woods, digging and scraping.

We worked all night till about eight the next
morning. We'd only had one quart canteen of
water apiece, and everybody was dying thirsty.
Our relief came in, so we started hiking the three
miles down to the Kaweah, where our truck was
waiting. Everybody was tired and dirty, so the line
was pretty quiet as it swung steadily down along
the trail. The headband holding my light on was
sweaty and tight. The wire hung bouncing along
my ear and down through the collar of my filthy
shirt. I had a blister on my middle toe that
twinged with every step. Dirt and charcoal lay in
layers on my face and legs. I was thirsty as hell.
But for some reason, I felt wonderful . . . .

Gallows in the Sky

Smokejumper Camp, Redwood Ranger Station,
Siskiyou National Forest, Cave Junction, Oregon.
Mid-June, 1948.

It is the start of Day 6 of training for the
nine new recruits in this 30-man smokejumper
crew. For a week the new men have been getting
intense ground instruction in steerable, slotted
parachutes, jumps off the shock-tower, practice in
rope let-downs from a cable fifty feet up,
strenuous exercise---calisthenics, running, sawing
logs and bending their backs on "the torture rack."
All this has been to prepare them for the first of
seven training jumps---scheduled to start a couple
of days from now---out of the airplane into the
forest to fight fire the fastest way available. For
they all are trained firefighters and they have three
whole weeks to learn how to be parachute-firemen
for the U.S. Forest Service's Region 6 before the
fire season starts heating up in the Cascades and

Coast Ranges. All of the camp crew, including
squadleaders and their chief, are in the camp
mess-hall wolfing down another great breakfast of
peaches, flapjacks, biscuits, cereal, milk, bacon,
eggs, potatoes and coffee when the chunky Camp
Foreman Cliff Marshall gets up to speak. He
makes an effort not to sound like what he was just
four years before: an Army paratrooper first-
sergeant haranguing his troops.

"Good morning, gentlemen. I hope you are
enjoying your breakfast. I have an announcement
for you nine new trainees. Right after breakfast,
report to the loft to get your jump gear, check to
see that you have everything, then haul it and
yourself aboard that big green stakeside truck in
the yard by eight o'clock. At 8:05 that truck will
move out for the airport. Because this morning,
gentlemen, before ten o'clock, you're all going to
make your first Forest Service parachute jump."

For nine new men, all of whom were
expecting two more days of ground training before
this moment, the bacon and eggs suddenly lose
their appeal, and neck hairs start to rise.

"You'll be jumping out of the Noorduyn
Norseman. Three men to a stick, alphabetical
order. Spotters will be Nolan, Green and Courson
in that order. That is all."

At this time, just three summers after the
end of World War II, smokejumping is still in its
infancy---in its ninth summer in fact. As I dump
out my big canvas sack of gear onto the airport
tarmac, I'm wearing my own personal uniform of
the day: Kant Bust'em Frisco Jeans, long-sleeved

work shirt, marine fatigue hat, paratrooper boots---
with no hooks, to avoid snaring. The gear spilled
out on the tarmac is sturdy and new yet somehow
oddly primitive-looking. There is the wide belt
("the girdle") for hauling in your gut as you bounce
down through tree branches and hope they keep
on being springy and soft. There are the heavy
canvas jump pants with their strong stirrup crotch
protection to prevent unspeakable branch-
straddling accidents. [That would end being
macho in a hurry, wouldn't it.] There's the 100-
foot nylon rope in a tight coil that goes inside your
right leg pocket---for getting down out of these tall
Oregon trees. [How tall do those Douglas fir
grow? One hundred eighty to 250 feet! Well you
can always lengthen it out with your reserve chute
and its risers---and your chute harness and your
shirt and pants and underwear and bootlaces. And
then you can slide down the rest of the way on
bubblegum and sheer guts!] There are the leather
work-gloves for sliding down that rope and fighting
fire. There is the stout canvas jump jacket with
the padded elbows and that absurdly high collar.
And there is the sturdy chute harness itself that
holds it and you all together. But the most
primitive piece is that helmet.

     I look at the helmet closely as I prepare to
really use it for the first time. It is actually a 40's
style regulation leather football helmet---the old
kind with a few air holes in the crown and ear-
holes in the sides so you can hear the quarterback
calling his signals. It even has a short leather chin
strap to keep it in place during scrimmage.

     To this football helmet there has been added

a wire-grill facemask with a sponge-rubber chin
cup which makes the whole smokejumping process
possible. That facemask is great---to let you see
out and breathe but keep branches and twigs out
of your eyes and face on your way down into the
forest. The facemask is attached on a hinge at the
forehead area of the helmet and can swing up like
a knight's visor when you want it out of the way
temporarily before the final suit-up. But to hold
the mask down when you are ready to jump, two
small straps have been attached to the right and
left jaw areas. These fit into small buckles
attached behind the ear-surfaces of the helmet.
As I put this rig on I am quite eager to put
everything on right. When the time comes to
lower face-mask, I slip the jaw straps firmly into
the behind-the-ear buckles and then notice that the
original chin strap of the football helmet is still
hanging loose. So I fasten it too.

　　　When we are all suited up, the squadleaders
bring up gray chafing bags and extract from them
the main 28-foot backpack chutes and snap them
into our harnesses above the shoulders. Then they
pull out smaller olive-drab bundles with red rip-
rings and secure these 24-foot reserve chutes to
our chests. That's the one you use if the main
chute doesn't open. The one that doesn't steer
and that hits the ground harder but does save your
life.

　　　On top of each reserve, looking up at you as
you look down, is a leather sheath enclosing a
sharp hunting knife. The knife is secured in the
sheath with a leather flap and metal snap. That
knife is for emergency use in case you have the

rare parachute malfunction of a shroudline or 2 or
3 going over the top of the opening canopy and
causing it to assume the buxom "Mae West"
shape, and thus not be catching its full
complement of air on the descent. With 28
shroudlines on the main chute you can cut any
three of those lines which may be malfunctioning
and still come in on the remaining lines with no
increase in rate-of-fall. In a way it's reassuring. In
another way it's not. What if 5 or 6 shroudlines
malfunction? And why did they name them
shroudlines anyway?

Okay. Okay. But would you be here if it
wasn't a dangerous job? Hell no. Who wants to
sell shoes in the home town for the summer when
he can be paid to jump out of airplanes over
flaming mountains?

Now the burly wide-legged Noorduyn
aircraft---single-engined work-horse of the North---
with Don Moyers at the controls is thundering into
position. The side-door is off the plane for easy
egress, and a little aluminum step hangs below
that open cave above the tarmac. Squadleader
Bob Nolan---the dashing gambler from Reno---
wearing a flat backpack chute for his reserve, and
a cloth pilot's helmet with goggles still up on his
forehead---is checking us out.

"Remember, men, learn how to check your
buddy's harness and quick-release safety-catch,
and static line and breaker cords, and let him
check yours too. And keep your static line in your
right hand but over your elbow not under it. You
don't want that arm jerked right up over your head
on opening shock."

"You'll be going out one man at a time on
this first stick---from 1500 feet, which gives you
plenty of time to glide to the mark. When I give
the word, you'll hook up your static line to the
cable over the door, then get in the door in the
one-half kneeling position, left knee on the deck,
right foot out on this little step. Then keep your
eyes out on the horizon as you wait for the slap.
When the engine throttles back and the plane
slows, I will slap your shoulder hard, and you will
step on out, folding your arms across your reserve
as you have been taught. You know how to check
your risers. You know how to steer that chute.
You know how to plane. Closest man to the red X
wins today's nine-dollar pool. Now let's go!"

We in the first stick do all that checking, get
a final check-out by Nolan himself; he lines us up
in order saying, "Jenkins, on the rear of the bench!
Then Kaarhus! Then Moffitt!" We waddle toward
the plane in our heavy gear and scramble aboard.
The interior is a bare oblong of space up to the
pilot-and-copilot's cabin with a wooden bench
along the far side. We climb in, sit on that bench,
trying not to catch our chutes on anything, and
Nolan slides in in front of us and stalks catlike up
to the copilot's seat. Moyers rumbles us to the
end of the airstrip and roars us down the runway
into the air.

As we climb up over the timber and
farmlands and meadows of southwestern Oregon,
over the winding brown Illinois River and the gray-
paved highway with its green bridges, we are
churning with excitement and bravado and no little

fear. In a few minutes Moyers has the necessary
altitude and is over the jump site, a roomy green
meadow west of town with a few small figures of
men and a red X of streamers laid out as target.
Nolan stalks back from the copilot's seat, crouches
in the open roaring door without even holding on---
as if he would just as soon fall out as not and try a
one-chute emergency jump for a change---and as
Don drones us over the target Bob throws out a
small yard-diameter drift-chute to measure the
wind-drift this morning. After a long stare:

"Looks like about eight miles per hour, from
the northwest. A fine day for jumping, men. I
wish I was going with you."

"Okay. Jenkins first. Collar up. Snap on
your static line right here!" I do so. His eyes and
hands are checking me out once more. "Now
move into the door."

From 1500 feet the country is green and
beautiful with Mungers Butte and Roundtop
between us and the valley of the Rogue. I take a
quick look down at the approaching meadow and
the little farm buildings and green trucks far below;
and then get a grip on the sides of the door, and
put my face in the buffeting wind and my right
foot out on the step as instructed. [That wind is
85 mph. Why do you suppose I'm sweating?] I
try to concentrate on the mountained horizon to
keep the sweat out of my eyes.

Suddenly on Bob's signal the engine goes
almost quiet and the wind slacks off to 65. "Now
watch that second step. It's a long one." Nolan
belts me on the shoulder and I stagger out the
door into the cyclone, arms folding over that

reserve. There is a long sickening feeling of
falling, then WHAM comes the opening shock.

But it's not the way an opening shock is
supposed to be as done off the shock-tower.
Suddenly I have been jerked upward by the back-
right part of my helmet, slashed across the chin by
the metal edge of the facemask and find myself
choking, one-quarter-inch from <u>hanging</u> in the chin
strap of the helmet.

Even though this is my very first parachute
jump, I know something is wrong---because I'm
looking out the ear-hole of the helmet.

The first thing I do---completely on reflex---is
rip that chin strap off my throat. Enough of this
gallows humor! Now I can feel the situation more
clearly, and I start batting my gloved hand against
what is still trying to pull my head out of its
socket: the right-rear part of that helmet. I begin
to realize what has happened: Somehow as I hit
the end of the static line---and the chute started
unreeling off my back---that high collar of the suit-
jacket flopped down in the wind, and <u>one shroud-
line</u> out of those 28 got caught under that little
buckle behind my right ear---and <u>I took the whole
opening shock on that one shortened shroudline
and buckle</u>.   Shroudline indeed!

The train of adrenalin-charged thought then
goes like this: Got to get this tangled line
unhooked so I can swing free on <u>all</u> the risers. [So
with gloved hand I paw at it again.] Not unhooked
yet. [Try again.]   Still no good. Okay. You can
cut any 3 tangled lines with the knife on the
reserve. Better get that knife out. [As I start to

do this another thought hits.]   But you're wearing
gloves. Can you get that sheath open and the
knife out with gloves on? Better take off the
gloves. [But before I can move:] But if I take
them off, I may lose them and need them later
down below to slide down that rope out of a tall
tree. So get that knife out with gloves on. But
before going through all that let's try once more
with gloved hand to get that wretched shroudline
unhooked. [And that time does it---and I swing
free into normal descent.]

Chief foreman and riggers on the ground are
all watching each of us closely as we exit the
plane. None see any malfunction as my turn
comes. So they conclude later that all of the
above anguished vacillation must have occurred in
about five seconds---since the chute assumed its
normal shape before anyone saw that near fatal
one-shroudline distortion. I believe them. A mind
under adrenalin and fear searches for answers like
lightning.

With the chute open right at last I have the
immense exhilaration of parachute flight. Shining
white nylon dome above. No lines over. Country-
side floating below with tiny cars on the highway
and cows in the fields. Now watch the speed of
drift and locate the red X. Wind pushing me
sideways so turn into it and plane. Can't hit the X
from where I'm drifting, but will be hitting the
meadow in fine shape. Wonderful to see the trees
and grass and little running people coming up.
There goes the bull horn. Must be Cliff

Marshall. What is he saying? Must be, "Okay, Jenkins. Let up on your planing and turn around. You're doing fine. Put your feet together and hang limp."

"Fall whichever way your body wants to roll."

"Limp as a sack. Feet together."

"That's it. Dump air from both slots just before you hit."

The trees are coming up fast but are all out of reach. The grass comes up faster and limp as a sack I whomp into the ground and roll over to pull on the cords of the quickly-collapsing chute.

"Okay! You did it!" And the new feeling of joy and exhilaration and "Hey, I want to do that again!" sweeps over me.

One of the riggers is running up to help me sack up that chute. As I pull off my helmet he says, "Hey. What the hell. Your chin is bleeding like a stuck pig! Here. Here's a bandanna."

"Yeah I had a little trouble up there. Almost hung in that goddam chin strap!"

"Chin strap? You mean your helmet still had a chin strap?"

"That's right. And I also got caught by one shroudline on this mask-buckle for my whole opening shock."

"Yikes. Hey. We better get you to a doctor."

So it is a free ride to the hospital in Grants Pass where the good Dr. Ogle sews up my chin with seven stitches. Then I have to lay out of the daily training jumps for a week while the old hide

heals. [And forever after I will wear that scar
proudly as a sign, Yes, you were brave enough to
jump---and whenever I shave the stubble from that
rumpled chin, I will think fondly of Cave Junction
and smokejumping.]

That puts me behind everyone else except
for one other man who twists an ankle later in the
week. And that gives me a great catch-up
schedule the following week. Two jumps on
Monday. And <u>four</u> jumps on Tuesday.

This provides one of the finest Tuesdays of
a madcap youth. About which more anon.

The Greatest Thrill of Them All

Pony Express riders, knights of old, mountaineers scaling Mount Everest or modern-day jet-fighter pilots---none have a more exciting job to do than the U.S. Forest Service smokejumpers. Smokejumpers are airborne firemen who parachute into wilderness timberstands of the West to fight forest fires. Tumbling from an airplane into wild mountain country thick with forests is all in a day's work for these men, who are trained to get to the ground safely, retrieve their gear from the treetops if necessary, put out the fire with simple hand tools, and hike out to civilization, with or without trails.

Parachuting to fires is simply the fastest, cheapest way to get fresh men and equipment in to much of the remote country of our western national forests, and as such it saves Uncle Sam hundreds of thousands of dollars each year in fire suppression costs. One fireboss, fighting a 160 acre fire in Montana with several types of crews, expressed it well as he radioed for more help: "Send me 50 more men or 25 more smoke-jumpers."

The work is far from all glamor and excitement. There is many a tedious labor detail between fires and many an exasperating "dry run" to a fire that cannot be located again in the vastness of the mountains. And, like all firemen, the smokejumpers spend most of their duty waiting, and trying to keep alert and ready. But when the fire call comes, as it does often in a tough fire season, with lightning lacing the mountains of the West, the smokejumpers have their magnificent moments.

I'd like to tell you about one that happened to me when I was being trained as a smokejumper in Cave Junction, Oregon, southern jumper base for the Forest Service's Northwestern Region (Region 6). It was not on a fire jump, but during what they called a slip jump, a harrowing all-out maneuver to help save your life in certain fire-jump emergencies. These might crop up if, as you leaped someday, the wind shifted strongly and began pushing you---despite all you could do with the forward speed and steering slots of the chute---toward such hazardous landings as:

---A deep cold lake (where 70 pounds of chutes, harness, letdown rope, logging boots, football helmet, and heavy canvas suit would almost certainly drown you).

---A sheer cliff of rock, or a porcupine slope of ugly snags (dead trees)---tall brittle daggers for a man or parachute to come down into.

---A roaring, rock-studded river like the Salmon or the Snake.

To avoid these dangers you were taught to pull a slip, which involved climbing three of the 28 suspension lines holding you to the canopy, until the great bubble of silk was pulled half over on its side, dumping much of its air, so that you would fall faster---and straight down---instead of drifting with the wind into whatever terror awaited you. The theory was that after falling far enough to get under the hazardous drift, you would let out on the slip slowly in order to put the chute back into normal shape for a landing. Five hundred feet was minimum altitude for any slip---to allow room for that vital restoration of the shiny cloth dome.

Things that made a slip jump tough were these:

I. The sheer physical difficulty of climbing hand-over-hand up three slender cords of slippery nylon---with gloves on, and with 60 pounds of gear freighting your body.

2. The higher you climbed on the lines, the more slack was left in them. Big, dangling arcs swung along your front, ready to tangle with your legs or boots or any of the lumpy projections on your reserve chute---and perhaps let you down into the trees back- or head-first if you got hopelessly snarled.

3. The faster fall meant you had to keep a sharper eye on the bristly ground below, to see that you didn't smack into it before letting out the lines.

4. The odd cobra-hood shape of the distorted chute caused it to twirl as it fell, carrying

you around with it. You had to be careful it didn't twirl faster than you did, and twist up into an impossible-to-unravel skein of death.

Because of these difficulties, the practice slip was made not from the usual 1,000 foot fire-jump altitude but from 2,200 feet, to give novices time to operate.

The day I made my slip jump was a sunny Tuesday in July, a Tuesday I'll always remember. I had been slightly injured on my first leap of the seven training jumps all parachute-firemen candidates must make to qualify. Hence I was behind the other trainees by almost a week. This day was calm and beautiful; and Foreman Cliff Marshall, a husky ex-paratrooper top-sergeant, decided to clean up all the stragglers on his training program while the weather held. This meant that the other man due to fly with me that day would be making two parachute jumps, and I would be making four.

The second one for both of us was to be the slip jump.

The plane was a single-engined Norseman, rugged aerial workhorse of the north country. With a door off you were right out there in the blast from the very take-off. After gaining altitude and hooking on our static lines, we moved to the doorway, the other man leading off. Obedient to Cliff's spotting, he stepped from the suddenly-quiet airplane at 2,200 feet. We circled and watched him struggle in vain to haul himself up the lines into a slip.

I sat there creaking in my gear, eyes riveted through the roaring door of the plane, tensed up

and puzzled, because I knew Jack, a logger most
of the year, was a far stronger man then I, and he
was failing. Jack, whom Marshall had given very
little offset for drift in anticipation of a good slip,
was sailing far beyond the jump-area pasture, out
over the trees, out and away into a dismal,
dangerous landing in a bend of the Illinois River
below. After a tense tight-circling moment, with
Jack's chute bellied full of current that was trying
to drown him in a deep pool, we watched him drag
himself out onto the bank and finally give us a
belated okay signal.

My turn next. I crouched in the doorway,
with one foot out on a little aluminum step hanging
there in space. Marshall, in his goggles and
emergency chute, checked my static line and a
dozen details of my harness rig. He lined up the
approach with signals to the pilot, and as the
engine throttled down to a mutter, gave me the
slap that meant "On your way!"

I stepped out and felt that strange
downrushing sensation of my body being sucked
toward earth. The backpack cracked open with its
old reassuring ecstasy, and I was soon checking
the shimmering nylon canopy for fouled lines. All
clear above. Oriented on the jump-zone below.
Okay, this is a slip jump. Better start to climb.

I singled out three lines from the splay
coming in above my right shoulder and started
taking little 6 in. bites on the collected strand,
knuckles on top before breaking over. The gloves
were gripping fine (God bless Bill Padden for
loaning me his good pliable ones); but I soon could
feel every foot getting harder. The skirt was

sagging, buckling, beginning to come down. Come on, Jenkins; you can do it. Dominate this monster!

Suddenly the chute started to spill air. I could feel it begin rushing past my ears till there was nothing but a tremendous hissing sound, getting louder every second. Better look down to see how fast the earth is coming up. Well, it's coming up all right, but there is still plenty of time. Look, the ground is beginning to wheel around too. That means your chute is doing the wheeling. Better keep your eye on it.

I looked up, to see that the chute was a great bucking banner in the sky, rumpling and booming as its tortured half-self cried out at this distortion. The twirling motion had started all right, and the slack lines were inching farther below my feet with every hoist.

Finally I reached a place somewhere just below the climactic point that takes the greatest effort, but I could climb no further. The burden on the arms was fantastic---like hanging onto a runaway sail that had somehow been torn into the sky by a hurricane. My head was bobbing up and down, scanning the wheeling canopy above and the rising earth below---the mountains and timber, and the beautiful green meadow and brown snaky river, and the grey highway slashing away through the trees. My heart was churning with excitement and my stomach rigid with fear, but somehow through it all I felt wonderful---and knew I would never live a more breathtaking moment then this.

The earth was rising as if in a vast invisible zoom lens, my arms were aching but triumphant at having conquered the slip; the hiss in my ears was drowning all but the booming reports of the nylon that flapped so fiercely 6 feet above me. Better let her out now. I can eat into that final five hundred feet in a hurry at this rate. Careful of those slack lines. Don't catch one on that boot stirrup. Paying them out is easy and fairly fast if I'm careful. There; she's almost down. Let her go and swing free. I'm on a normal jump now. Swing into the wind and plane a little for the landing. That's plenty to reach the center of the meadow. Now face around to come in frontwards. Feet together, arms overhead. Limp as a sack I whump into the firm grass and collapse into a happy mass of tangled cordage. Slip jump completed!

The slip jump has been eliminated from the smokejumper's training for a good many years now. Too dangerous; plus the fact that there's considerable evidence that it doesn't accomplish what it's supposed to---that the pulled-down canopy acts like a sail, carrying you along <u>with</u> the wind and nullifying the very escape from a perilous drift that it is intended to provide. But I personally am yet to be fully convinced that the marvelous falling climb through the sky doesn't work. For when the wind roars your ears into deafness except for that flapping boom overhead, it doesn't seem possible that a cross-wind would have much effect over the giant homing force of gravity.

I could be wrong. Bill Wood, veteran firefighter and the Forest Service's aerial research man at Missoula, Montana, is convinced. Bill ran the tests to see which was more effective in escaping a deadly drift, a slip jump or a 100 per cent job of planing---tilting the front of the chute down slightly to jet air out the rear, with steering slots and tails giving even more of a push---to within 50 feet of the ground. Two men jumped in like conditions, trying the two methods. When they hit, Bill was convinced that, with all its dangers, the slip jump wasn't worth the difference. So you won't find the smokejumpers doing it any more---and certainly nobody else. Thus the slip jump remains in a forgotten eddy of history, merely a stunt now, perhaps to scare the heart out of an occasional air show crowd---a bygone foray with a windmill, by men who should have had their heads examined anyway.

But if you're one of those men or women who have been everywhere and done everything and the world is stale for adventure, you might try this to liven up a Sunday afternoon---a slip jump from 2000 feet over some great burning chasm in the mountainous Northwest.

Baptism of Johnny O'Neill

It all started last winter when the Forest Service wheels decided they needed twenty jumpers working out of Dog Flat to really protect this part of the Cascades. Redwood used to take care of all the wilderness fires up this way; but this year, since they have to cover all of northern California too, they don't have enough men or planes to handle the back-country lightning strikes up here. The wheels picked Dog Flat because of its airstrip and because there was a barn behind the ranger station they could convert into a parachute loft with no strain. Then they began shipping in chutes and sewing machines and jump suits and helmets and all the thousand-and-one other things a smokejumper camp needs. Somebody hauled a bunch of tent-platforms up from an old BRC camp in the valley; and I guess they built the mess hall new. But by May 1, things were beginning to shape up, and the fire-control office in Portland was looking for someone to run the outfit.

The guy they picked was Johnny O'Neill, a blond hard-muscled little squadleader from Redwood, where we both used to work. Johnny's had plenty enough experience to be a foreman--- four years in the troops during the war, and three years since as year-round jumper and squadleader both at Missoula and Redwood---and he taught me all I know about packing chutes. He's got the quickest, surest judgment in the air I've ever seen and can handle one of those slotted chutes almost like a glider, putting himself down practically anywhere he wants to. And he can spot guys out of a plane so they'll land right where he needs 'em on a fire.

Johnny's a terror for hard work too. A couple of times I've seen him dig fire trail thirty-six hours straight, without stopping except to eat. There isn't a better aerial fire-suppression man in the Forest Service; and it's no wonder Portland decided he should run the Dog Flat show. Johnny's wiry and slight, and he has a blond crewcut and boyish face with freckles. At twenty-five he's the youngest jump foreman the Forest Service's ever had; and because of that the wheels who appointed him are keeping a mighty sharp eye on him.

Anyway they upped him to an SP-8 rating, gave him a single-engined Norseman (with Duke Wilson to pilot it), and let him pick two experienced riggers from anywhere in the region as his squadleaders. That's how me and Art Hodes happen to be working here this year. We came up with Johnny early in June and worked like ants to get things organized before the new men arrived

for the fire season---July through September. A
cook and a flunky came with us, and a non-
jumping clerk to keep the books. And a week later
a light recon plane arrived with a two-man crew,
and we were almost complete.

The first half of the jump crew---new men
who had to be trained from scratch---came in June
15; and we took our refresher jumps as
demonstrations and began putting the fellas
through their ground training. There were nine of
'em, mostly college guys off for the summer, and
one or two loggers out for a thrill. A good bunch
all told, with some pretty rugged builds among
them. It was funny, the first day to see the looks
on their faces when little Johnny came out and
started signing them in. I guess they expected all
smokejumpers to be brutes and the foreman to be
the biggest ogre of all. But Johnny just shook
hands all around and got the papers squared away
and told them each to pick a bunk in one of the
tents before getting fitted with jump suits in the
loft.

During the ground training though the new
guys began to realize why such a slim young-
looking fella as Johnny could be foreman of what
they expected to be one hellishly tough outfit.
Johnny could do calisthenics longer than any man
in camp; and on our three-mile runs every day he'd
finish ahead of everybody---even the college track
men who thought they were in shape. And when
he demonstrated the emergency slip-jump, that
was the clincher.

Johnny went out at eighteen hundred feet,
spotting himself so he'd have to slip to hit the

field; and he did a slip that'd take your breath away. We could see his canopy dimple and then sag over and start flapping as he climbed three of the shroud lines to half collapse the chute and speed up his rate of fall. The canopy was twirling, and falling faster and faster, and Johnny was just a little black speck clinging to the very skirts of the bucking canopy---and he was getting bigger every second. He eased out of the slip at five hundred feet and then planed like a gull to get over the target. He made it with sixty feet to spare and braked his speed by spilling both slots at once. Then he hung limp and hit the ground in an easy roll, draping his canopy right over the marking-streamers. That's great jumping in any man's language.

As you've probably gathered by now, Johnny O'Neill was a pretty capable guy. In fact, before we started that first bunch on their seven practice jumps, he looked like he'd make a perfect smokejumper foreman. That's because nobody knew what funny kind of nerves Johnny had. Not that you could faze him by putting him in a rough spot alone---the way smokejumpers always seem to be getting in jams. Because with only himself to worry about, Johnny knew his own skill and muscle and will-to-live would take care of him; and he just didn't know what fear was. But give him a $30,000 airplane and a pilot and two or three inexperienced men to be responsible for in the air, and he'd go white under his freckles and begin sweating like the greenest recruit ever to make a first jump.

When Johnny was alone, he was absolutely

the bravest or craziest or most indifferent man I
ever knew. I've seen him climb 180 feet in a doug
fir to retrieve a cargo chute and go up with no
more concern than if he was climbing a flight of
stairs. And last year when his chute streamed on
that free-fall he did at the Rogue River Air Show, it
didn't panic him a bit. He just rode the stream
down a thousand feet, hoping it would flatten and
catch air so he would land easy with the big
canopy. But when it still hadn't opened four
hundred feet from the ground, he pulled his reserve
and came in harder on the little one. Half the
women in the crowd fainted before he cracked
that emergency chute; and when he landed,
everybody was quaking and scared silly. All
except Johnny. He picked himself up, grinning like
a cat at the poor frightened crowd, and started
calmly undoing his harness and putting his chutes
into a sack.

    But it was a different story when he had
people besides himself to watch out for. I don't
know if all jump foremen go through the same kind
of hell Johnny did when they start; but I know I
wouldn't want the extra thirty bucks a month to
handle all that worry. He's got the whole show
checked out to him---thousands of dollars' worth
of chutes and tools and webbing and sewing
machines; all those buildings and tents he's
responsible for; two stakeside trucks and a pickup;
the planes, and, not least of all, twenty guys
working on all kinds of skittish jobs, from falling
snags to stringing telephone wire. If anybody
makes a mistake anywhere down the line, jumping,
or rigging, or just backing a truck into the side of

the loft, Johnny has to take the rap. Naturally that
kind of strain began to make him edgy. But from
knowing him before, I didn't think he'd come as
close to crackin' as he did.

　　We didn't find out about Johnny's nerves till
the new men were ready for their first jump. Of
course, we let them think they had another day or
two of rope letdown practice first, so they could
sleep the night before. But then at breakfast
Johnny got up and told them they were going to
jump that morning so they better check their gear
again and be ready to go. Well, most of them
didn't want any more breakfast then, and they all
left the cookshack early to go over their suits and
harnesses; and their first-jump nerves began to
make Johnny sweat along with them.

　　Out on the strip, while Duke Wilson was
making a heck of a racket warming up the plane,
Johnny was walking around white-faced and wet,
checking each new man a half a dozen times to
make sure his harness and backpack and reserve
were on right. I was amazed, because I'd never
seen Johnny scared before, and I couldn't figure
out why he took so long going over the guys---
when he knew I had already checked the safety-
catches on the quick-release plates I dunno how
many times. If the new guys standing around
hadn't been so nervous, I would have ribbed
Johnny about it. But looking back, I don't think it
would have improved matters any; and I'm glad I
didn't.

　　They went up in three sticks of three men
each, and everybody got into the field okay except
Oshevski, who hung in a tree and had to make a

forty-foot letdown. Newhouse and Johnson tied
for the prize-money (that they all chip in for each
jump) by both landing twenty paces from the
mark. Johnny was mighty shot when that morning
was over. He was just exhausted from nerves,
and I still couldn't understand why. He talked
about it that afternoon while we were packing the
chutes in the loft, and finally I began to catch on
to what was wrong. Johnny finished with, "I
don't know what's happened to me, Pete. I can't
seem to get the old charge out of going up. Not
when I know all those lives and equipment are
checked out to me---and me alone."

"Yeah," I said, moving up the table
straightening suspension lines, "I guess it's a lot
simpler when you just have day-to-day work-
details to handle, instead of the whole shootin'
match." Then I added, "If there's anything I can
do---?"

"No, Pete. Thanks. I guess I'll just have to
sweat it out. It probably won't be so bad
tomorrow."

Well, it was worse the next day instead of
better. Johnny was absolutely shaking when he
climbed into the plane with his spotter's chute and
goggles on. The three new men in the plane were
sitting there stiff and quiet on the bench, their
helmets and high-collared suits lost in the gloom of
the plane. They weren't joking either, the way
guys usually do when they're trying to keep up
their nerve for a jump.

Johnny put the guys out all right (because
spotting is just about automatic with him), but he
told me that afternoon that he'd almost let

Oshevski jump with the static line under his arm. And I can tell you, from a jump like that I made down in the Siskiyou once, a static line under the arm can be mighty painful. The chute goes out under your arm instead of off your back, and the opening shock of all twenty-eight lines smashes that arm from below and yanks it up behind your head like a sledge-hammer had hit it. I was lucky. My arm didn't break. But I was black-and-blue from my chest to my elbow for three weeks after.

Johnny and I were in the loft again, talking as we worked, and Art Hodes had the rest of the camp out with belts and spurs practicing tree climbing. I was shaking-out the last of nine chutes they'd used that morning and listening to Johnny talk about the jump.

"Those kids did pretty well for just their second time," he said, unrolling a chute on the long table. "Brian is mighty sharp on his planing, though his drift-judgment's not too good yet." He combed the lines and ruffled the silk expertly, in case a stray twig was still caught in the folds.

"Who took the pot this morning?" I asked, figuring it wouldn't hurt Johnny to talk some of the tightness out of his system.

"Newhouse, that ex-trooper. Fourteen paces. Beat out Brian by five or six yards."

"Have any freezes in this bunch yet?" I knew damn well he hadn't but I wanted him to see how bright things really were.

"Nope. Johnson looked awful green on the ground yesterday before the jump. But he went out like a dream when the time came.

I thought I was doing it. Calming him down by getting his mind off that aching load of responsibility. His face looked easy and relaxed as he began working the lines carefully through the loops of the backboard. He looked almost like the Johnny O'Neill I'd once known. Confident, hard-working, with quick sure movements and a drive in everything he did. He finished folding the canopy and slipped the whole shimmering wad of fabric onto the press and popped it up into the elastic-edged chute-cover with a quick thrust of his foot.

"There," he said. "Six more and we're done."

I didn't see the guys take off in the morning. I was at the jump field laying out three orange signal streamers in a big asterisk for the guys to aim for. It wasn't long till the Norseman droned into sight and the driftchutes came out and I could see somebody's foot on the step as the plane came around again. That would be Oshevski if I had the jump order right. Third practice jump; thirteen hundred feet; and hundred feet lower than yesterday. I saw his chute blossom and saw it twirl as he tugged a guideline, and he started planing toward the mark against the wind. He was working hard to avoid the timber this time, and his canvas suit was yellow in the sun. The sky was bright blue against the shining beauty of the chute, and when he was a hundred feet from the ground I megaphoned my hands and began talking him down.

"Feet together!" I yelled, as loud as I could holler. "Hands on the risers! And stop planing at fifty feet!" I was sprinting across the field to keep

up with him, and he was sailing diagonally down,
oscillating slightly in the wind.

"Hands on the risers!" I yelled again.
"Relax as you hit." Then just in time I reminded
him, "Feet together!"

I was mighty relieved when he thumped into
the grassy turf thirty yards ahead of me and came
up out of his roll with a happy yell. He started
waving OKAY with his signal streamers as soon as
he'd collapsed his chute; and I was running toward
him to help him out of his gear.

Somehow I thought that was good luck.
Oshevski had made it down safe and was almost
close enough to the mark to compete for the nine-
dollar pot. The rest of the stick came down nice,
and the Norseman went back for more, and I was
feeling good. Newhouse came out clean as first
man of the second stick; and he looked like he was
going to hit the spot square, but a gust caught him
two hundred feet up and blew him off almost to
the edge of the timber. Now Brian had his chance,
I thought, for I knew he was next; and I waited for
him to come out on the following pass. The plane
went silent like it always does, and I waited to see
the chute crack open. But the plane started up
again and nothing happened.

Then I saw Brian, a black tumbling body
about eight hundred feet off the ground, growing
like a flack-burst as he fell.

His chute was still on his back! I hardly
realized it before his reserve sprouted in a
comforting dome and I could breathe again; and I
started running toward where he would land. He
lit pretty hard with just a twenty-two foot chute,

and the way he crumpled into the ground I thought
he'd never get up. But he did, and said he was
okay, and there was a tight washed-out grin of
relief on his handsome face.

First thing I did was unsnap the bad chute---
which was one of the set we had put up the day
before. It was a thick white lump of matted silk
that had somehow kept itself from catching air
during his six hundred feet of free fall. The cover
was gone, so the static line must have worked all
right. And I guessed that the break-cord had
caught on something in the plane and broken
before he jumped. I took the chute's record card
from its slot in the backboard and put it in my
pocket without looking at it. Because I was afraid
Brian might be bitter at whoever had packed that
chute; and I knew only one of two guys had
packed it. Johnny O'Neill or me.

Parachutes are funny animals. Most all the
time they open. But once in a while they don't.
There doesn't have to be a reason why they do
one or the other. They just do. You can pack 'em
perfect---and you don't rig unless you do---without
ever knowing for sure that they'll open. Nobody
can tell. That's why you wear two: a backpack
main chute that's pretty sure to open, and a
chestpack reserve that's pretty sure to open, if the
other one doesn't.

You can pack ten thousand parachutes
that'll sprout like dreams and never be sure the
next one you pack won't stream or stay on the
guy's back or roll him up in a big silk shroud. It
depends on a lot of things. The static line for
instance, a big strong length of webbing that jerks

the cover off the chute as the jumper drops away
from the plane. Or the break-cord, a little piece of
string that pulls the chute out full length before the
guy's weight snaps it free from the cover.
Sometimes the air has funny effects, the way it
moves, and what it's made of that day---like water
maybe. Or the way the jumper rolls and twists as
he falls. How the nylon feels just then, or the silk.
Whether it feels like jumping out into the
turbulence or just lying there in a lump waiting for
the guy to burn in. But there doesn't have to be a
reason.

   The record card had Johnny O'Neill's name
on it. I admit I felt relieved as hell that I hadn't
been the one, but I knew Johnny would really
suffer for having packed that chute. Not from
Brian of course or the guys in camp (because I was
going to do my damndest to keep them from
finding out); and not even so much from regional
headquarters. Where Johnny would suffer was
inside, feeling guilty about something he didn't
have to feel guilty about. Tying himself in a knot
over what might have happened, and thinking he
was a rotten leader who didn't deserve the respect
of his men. Worst of all, it would wreck whatever
chance he had of getting his old courage back,
courage to run this outfit the way he used to
handle himself.

   As soon as the Norseman was back on the
ground, Johnny knew the score from the chute-
numbers in the jump log; and the guilt I was afraid
of began eating into him. Of course, Art Hodes,
who was keeping the log that morning, knew who
had packed that chute, too; but Art is a deadpan

and a hell of a good man to keep a secret. We couldn't keep it a secret from our overhead though. Anything like a man coming down on his reserve has to go in Johnny's work-diary and be explained to regional headquarters in triplicate. And the whole town of Dog Flat knew somebody's chute hadn't opened that day.

That really put Johnny on probation with the wheels, and we began getting inspection visits at all hours to see that we were on the ball. The added pressure made Johnny worse instead of better, and he started sluffing all the roughest parts of his job onto me and Art Hodes. We packed all the chutes, did all the pre-jump checking, managed the refresher firefighting, and Art spotted the rest of Group One's practice jumps. Johnny would stay in his office doing paper work most of the time and come out once in a while to put assignment sheets on the bulletin board.

I didn't like that. Not because of the extra work I had to do. But it looked to me like Johnny was backing off, running away from the toughest problem he'd ever come up against. I'd never seen him turn tail from anything before, and I wanted to grab him by the shoulders and shake him and yell "That's not the way, Johnny. You can't get away from it that way!"

Not that Art Hodes and I couldn't handle those last four practice jumps all right---Art in the air and me on the ground. We'd even take care of the second batch of new men, too, if need be---the ones that were due in a week later. Art is plenty good as a spotter. He's a lanky salty old ex-

trooper with fifty-six jumps in, and he doesn't give
a damn for anything. He always needs a shave
even though he's good looking in a rough sort of
way; and his favorite trick to scare the new men is
to hang by one hand from the static cable---out in
the slipstream from the waist up---while he looks
over the ground and gets the drift. And when the
time comes to slap the guys on the shoulder, he
never gives any pep talk except maybe, "Watch
that second step; it's a long one," or, "Now get
the hell out of here." The guys like him though,
and we didn't have any trouble.

The last batch of recruits came in July 1,
eight of them that time; and we started putting
them through their two-and-a-half weeks of
training. I guess Johnny had planned to have Art
spot them on all their jumps, but the day of the
first one we got a surprise call from Portland
saying that some of the wheels were coming out
to watch the jump and would we please hold it in
the afternoon instead of the morning. That was
bad for everybody, announcing the jump to a
bunch of green guys and then putting it off six
hours. The new guys sweated all morning, and
Johnny put them out buck-sawing logs to keep
them occupied. He even took a half-hour on a saw
himself to keep from knotting up like the recruits,
but it didn't work; and finally he went back and
started straightening up the loft and waiting.

He knew as well as I did that the wheels
were coming out more to check on him than to see
the jump; and he began sweating-out whether he
should spot or let Art do it. The state Johnny was
in, he knew old nonchalant Art would do a much

safer job. But it wouldn't look right to the higher-ups to see Johnny stay on the ground while one of his squadleaders put the new men through their first jump. I wanted Johnny to tackle it, even though I tried not to think about what might happen if he did.

At two o'clock Johnny was pacing up and down along the apron, still undecided. Duke Wilson had warmed the Norseman's engine for ten minutes and then shut it off; and things were awfully quiet along the strip as we waited. The new guys were suited up and sitting on the steps of the hangar, smoking and nervously checking their harnesses; and way across town you could hear a sawmill scream in the hot afternoon. The first three guys had their chutes on already and their facemasks down, and one of them kept putting on his gloves and taking them off again.

One other guy especially was so jittery it was pathetic. His name was Flynn, a big guy from Texas, and he had an elastic-bungee on his helmet that held the facemask up off his face---so he looked like an old knight with his visor raised before going into battle. Flynn didn't look in any shape for a battle though. His face was dead-white and moist-looking, and he kept wiping the sweat off his mouth with the sleeve of his jump jacket. He sat there chainsmoking cigarettes; and the cigarettes wobbled in his fingers, and his lips quivered constantly between drags. I thought at the time it was too bad he was slated for the last stick---and would have to sweat the longest of anybody. He'd smile a flat hollow smile every time somebody looked at him; but there wasn't anything but fear in that smile; and I hoped Johnny wouldn't notice him. Finally a sleek green panel-truck with a tall radio aerial swung up the yellowdust road to the strip, and we knew the wheels from Portland had arrived.

Johnny's face was bleak to look at when he saw the truck coming. Because he knew the decision couldn't be put off any longer. He turned suddenly to Art and said raspily, "I'll take them up, Art. You go over to the jump field and talk 'em down." Johnny O'Neill was forcing himself to do what by now frightened him more than anything else in the world---to spot a stick of jumpers he was responsible for out of a plane. His hands shook as he took the flatpack from Hodes and started buckling it on, and he faked a grin at me and said, "You might as well come along, Pete. I've got to start checking you out on spotting sometime."

He was right. I needed to learn that end of the game. But I think he wanted me along more for moral support than to give me a spotting lesson. And right then I was glad I was Johnny O'Neill's friend.

The wheels were getting out of their panel then and shaking hands all around, and Johnny was doing his best to be amiable. There was Partridge, the Forest Supervisor, a little pot-bellied guy in khaki; and a tall gray-haired man I recognized as Jacobs, fire-control officer of the whole region. The other two guys with them were bigwigs from Washington who had never seen aerial fire-suppression men before. They had to have everything explained to them---all about the

economy of hitting wilderness fires from the air
while they're still small, and the use of every piece
of equipment a jumper wears, what tools and
equipment go into a firepack, and so forth---till we
were ready to pop. They stood out there with one
of the suited-up guys asking questions about this
and that till I was afraid Johnny'd tell 'em all to go
to hell. It was almost three o'clock before they'd
let us go ahead with the jump.

Finally I scooted up to the co-pilot's seat
beside Duke, and the first stick staggered toward
the plane and climbed aboard. Johnny looked bitter
in spite of himself as he broke away from the
visitors and ran for the plane. But he looked good
to me, taking us up again on his own. His crewcut
was fluttering in the propblast, and the white
straps of the flatpack were snug across his chest.
Duke revved her up and we took off, and as we
came back the downwind leg we could see the
panel-truck moving like a big green beetle toward
the jump field.

"They're going out to watch the landings
now," Duke yelled in my ear. "Let's hope to hell
nothing goes wrong."

I nodded and looked back at Johnny. He
was looking out at the bristly timbered ridges, his
lips a brittle line across his face---doing just what
any jumper does after he's checked everything
three times. Trying to get his mind off himself and
what might happen by looking at the scenery, or
the inside of the plane, or the road and the bridges
down below.

When we were over the field, Johnny
lowered his goggles and called me back to have

me run through the spotting with him, watching
the driftchutes go down and counting out the
distance in seconds. But I could see his mind
wasn't on teaching particularly; it was on the eight
new men he was going to put out that door---and
what would happen if anything went wrong in
front of all that Forest Service brass.

But the first stick went out fine. Good body
position on all three, and everybody made the field
okay. The green beetle got there in time to see
the first man land; and when we'd dumped the last
one, we went back for the second load.

"You're doing great," I yelled at Johnny, and
he grinned a little as he moved up toward the
pilot's cabin.

The second stick was good, too, and on the
last one (of only Coleman and Flynn) Johnny had
me down beside him to see how he checked the
guys over when they got in the door. Flynn, the
chainsmoker, was going out first, and I could see
the fear in his face as Johnny checked his static
line and the position of his hands and tugged at his
legstraps a last time. When Flynn was all set and
we were swinging in for our run on the field,
Johnny said to him, yelling to be heard above the
roaring wind, "Watch the wingtip as you go out,
and don't forget your body position." Then
through Flynn's wire mask Johnny noticed how
terror-stricken the guy looked, and Johnny's head
jerked like he'd been slapped across the mouth
with a brick. I was afraid he'd break down right
there and not be able to go on, but finally he
gripped himself hard and said to Flynn, "If you
don't want to jump, Flynn, say so. It won't be a

disgrace. Some guys just aren't built for this job, that's all."

Flynn shook his head. "Oh, no; I'll jump," he said. "I'm scared, sure. But who isn't their first time out?" He grinned that hollow grin. "I'll jump."

"Good boy," Johnny said, squeezing Flynn's arm. Then all of Johnny's attention was forward, on the field and the mark; and he was coaxing Duke Wilson into just the right path over the intercom mike. When he'd counted out the drift correction, Johnny snapped into the mike, "Cut!" and Duke throttled down to a dead sixty miles an hour. Then Johnny pounded Flynn on the shoulder---the signal to jump.

Flynn sat there without moving for two whole seconds, his face an ice-cold mask of tension; and the plane mushed down in a heavy glide as Duke waited for him to go. Finally Duke had to gun the motor again to keep the plane flying, and just then Flynn moved. He stood up on the step---the way a guy should going out---and the wind hit him hard. But then he couldn't face finishing it; and he half-turned back to the plane, screaming like a madman and clawing for his static line and the safety bar. His feet twisted off the step under him and his elbows bounced from the floor of the plane out onto the step. He kept slipping down till he was hanging by his hands from that little knurled piece of duraluminum, a foot below the plane and fifteen hundred feet above the earth. I lunged back to the door and looked down at him, Johnny and me shoulder to shoulder. Flynn's head was tilted toward us, and

he was crying like a baby under the wire grill of his
mask. And he twisted in the wind with his feet
trailing away behind us; and I couldn't hear him
crying for the roar of the plane.

You can imagine how scared the guy was
when you realize he was hanging by his fingers in
a ninety-mile gale with seventy pounds of
equipment on besides his own weight. Johnny
and I didn't have a chance in the world of getting
him back inside, not without dragging him over
that step and maybe cracking his reserve. Then
we'd have a runaway canopy wrapping up the tail
of the ship and wrecking it with all hands. It
doesn't take much of a disturbance to open one of
those reserves. Even the slipstream can do it; and
the way the blast was slamming Flynn around, any
second his reserve might blossom suddenly and
drag us all to hell.

Of course, Flynn's static line was hooked
up, and he had two chutes on. The safest thing
for him to do was let go and have the chute take
him down. But he was too terrified to try that,
and he looked up at us with the most pitiful
expression on his face that I ever hope to see.

Johnny had seen the danger to the plane
right off. He had been yelling down at Flynn, "Let
go! Let go!" but I doubt if the guy heard a thing
through that howling wind and the roar of the
engine. Even if he had heard, it wouldn't have
made any difference, not to a man as fear-crazed
as he was. Johnny's job right then was to bring
five guys and a $30,000 airplane back safe. So he
reached down and did the one thing that would
save us all.

He pried Flynn's fingers loose from the step.

Flynn went off shrieking, but his chute opened all right---even though we were miles beyond the field by that time. As we circled back by him we could see he wasn't raising a finger to steer his chute---just letting it drift with the wind till he disappeared in the timber behind us. We went back and dumped Coleman and radioed Art to start looking for Flynn two miles north in the timber. We found him an hour later, as conscious as you are, and without a mark on him. He was still in his chute harness, hanging about three feet off the ground and not making a sound. And he didn't remember a thing that had happened in the plane.

It may sound funny, but Johnny wasn't shaken by it a bit. Not that he didn't pity poor Flynn. It was just that Johnny was through shaking for awhile. Because he knew now that he could handle any emergencies we'd run into as well as he'd just handled Flynn. And he knew also, whether in a tight place or not, Johnny O'Neill was still running the Dog Flat crew.

Flynn left that afternoon, on the 5:30 bus. We all felt sorry for him, with what had happened, and we hoped he wouldn't brood about it too much on the long trip back to Texas. But shoving off was the only thing he could do. Like Johnny says, some guys just aren't built for this kind of a job, that's all.

After that though, Johnny had his job by the horns. He buckled down to the responsible parts of his work with the old O'Neill drive, and you could see his confidence coming back and the steady hand and eye he used to have. We finished out the practice jumps with no more mishaps, and I got checked out on spotting before we were through. Johnny was solid as a rock by the time Group Two had qualified as parachute-firemen, and that was a happy day for the whole camp. Johnny never got quite as careless with the men under him as he used to be with himself; but when he'd lead a rescue jump or follow us down on a big fire, I could see the old magic was still there.

It's a good thing, too, 'cause the fires have really been popping in the back-country this year. Looks like every man jack of us will clear a thousand bucks by October.

And our safety-records and reports-of action from other forests have been almost perfect this summer---thanks to a foreman like Johnny O'Neill.

Fire on the Shasta

It was Saturday afternoon and hot, and the men on standby at the smokejumper camp, Redwood Ranger Station, lay on their bunks and waited. All week long fire danger had been high; and with a thunderstorm moving down the Cascades, the men knew it was just a matter of time till back-country timber in any of a dozen national forests in Oregon or northern California would start smoking. Time, yes. But how much time?

At two o'clock the phone in the office rang. You could hear it clear across camp in the hot stillness; and men in the tents swung their feet softly to the floor as they counted out four rings. It was time for the usual gag-line of "Six men on the Umpqua!" that came every time the camp phone rang; but for some reason nobody said it. And we listened in the airless quiet as Foreman Cliff Marshall lifted the receiver.

A minute later Cliff's first-sergeant voice was booming across the campground. "Fire jump! Shasta again. Cummings, Foster, Jenkins! Get your gear!"

Shasta again! The same forest in northern Cal that Nolan and the boys got back from this morning! Geez, they must be burnin' to hell down there; and the storm hasn't even hit them yet.

Every man in camp poured out of the tents to help load the truck with firepacks and parachutes; and we, the top three on the jump list, sprinted to the aerial shack for our sacks of equipment. Padded canvas suit, football helmet with wire faceguard, quick-release harness, 100-foot rope for getting out of trees, orange signal streamers. They were all there, 'cause we'd checked them half a dozen times.

Cliff was phoning again, talking to the pilot and then to forest headquarters. Then he was out among us, handing Foster a map with the fire section marked on it and explaining, "They want twelve men, but we can only send 'em six because the fire danger here in the Siskiyou is too great. It's the same fire that Nolan and the guys went on on Thursday; but it's gotten away from the ground crew."

We thought of the haggard guys that came in about noon---Nolan, Block, and Barrett---and what they said about leaving the little lightning-strike trailed and dying at one eighth of an acre in the hands of a ground crew, and packing out on horses by moonlight eighteen miles to the nearest road. But how could that small a fire have gotten away from a six-man ground crew? And we

remembered Nolan saying the brush was so thick
that he and the others had struggled six-and-a-half
hours dragging ninety pounds each of chutes and
equipment <u>one little mile</u> to the trail and the
horses. [And it was reliably reported later that two
of those smokejumpers were quite nervous about
climbing aboard horses for the ride out.]

Cliff went on. "There'll be six of you, so
put extra sleeping bags and clackboards on those
firepacks. The second stick will be Fieldhouse,
Speaker, and Kaarhus. Another plane is on its way
from Redding to take you last three in. So we'll go
on as soon as we get loaded; and Foster, you'll be
in charge of all jumpers on the ground."

A last minute flurry of activity; and then we
piled on the truck and churned away toward the
airport. Back in the truckbed Foster, Cummings,
and I lurched around on a mountain of gear---gray
chafing bags that held a main and a reserve chute
each; squat firepacks, trim and tight with their load
of bedrolls, rations, and canteens (and with tool-
handles poking out the top); small canvas globes
that were the cargo chutes; and our own white-
sacked jump equipment.

A few minutes later part of our gear
mountain was being transferred into the plane
while we pulled on the big canvas suits. The
plane, a husky silver Noorduyn, was already
gassed up and ready. She swallowed two
firepacks, some cargo chutes, a guarded crosscut
saw, and a five gallon water drum; and Don
Moyer, the pilot, climbed in to kick over the
engine. Cliff scurried around excitedly, doing a
hundred jobs that had to be done. "Is the water in

those canteens fresh? Don't forget the drift
chutes. You remember where it is Don, twenty
miles south of Mount Shasta. How's the weather
down there?"

Foster stuffed a radio beside the rope in his
baggy legpocket, and Cummings carried the
climbing spurs and fannol saw in his. We put on
our harnesses, and then somebody was snapping
chutes into them and checking us out. We
watched carefully as the squadleader examined all
the details of our harnesses and reserves and
backpacks to make sure everything was right.
And it felt sort of chilly when Foster noticed---after
being checked out---that a bungee was missing
from his reserve. "Gee," he said looking at the
record card, "and packed by the old master, too."

Of course everybody makes mistakes. But
here a mistake can mean a life. Your life.

Foster got another reserve, and the three of
us staggered toward the plane in our seventy
pounds of gear, climbed in, and sat bulkily on the
bench along one wall. It was a tight fit with all the
cargo. I was squeezed close up behind the pilot,
with Cummings next to me; and Foster sat closest
to the yawning doorway. Cliff, who would be
spotting us out the door in an hour, crawled over
the cargo to the copilot's seat, and Don shoved
the throttle forward to take off.

Twenty minutes later we were above the
yellow Klamath River, and my leg was going to
sleep wedged against the firepacks in front of me.
Suddenly Mount Shasta was tall in the sky out to
the left, and we stared in wonder at its massive
green shoulders and snow-streaked summit.

Somebody pointed to a little town cross-hatched below and said, "That's Yreka." And a few minutes later, "That must be Weed."

We droned alongside a lookout tower that was perched on a perfectly conical little mountain rising from the flatland below. Then a yellow Waco climbed to meet us from Shasta City airport and led the way south over shaggy timbered ridges to the fire.

I looked over the pilot's shoulder, and pretty soon I could see smoke ahead, white smoke pouring up a mountainside. Little Shoemhorse Creek, Shasta National Forest. California, Region Five. The only western region besides Colorado that doesn't have its own jumpers yet. Cliff scrambled back to the broad roaring door, and we buckled down our facemasks and pulled on our gloves. Then we craned out the windows to see the ragged black scar on the ridge-spur below, close to fifteen acres by now and burning uphill briskly in the hot afternoon. There she was, a wilderness fire. What we'd trained and waited and hoped for four weeks. We were ready, but still a tingle of fear shot through us as we thought of jumping into lonesome, wild country like that, not knowing what was down below. And we looked around hard to get every possible advantage from knowing the terrain.

Don circled twice, and Cliff threw out yard-square drift chutes to get the wind. Then Foster hooked up and scooted forward to sit in the door. Chuck Foster, a second-year smokejumper; husky blond ex-marine, veteran of Iwo and Guadalcanal, now a forestry major at Oregon State.

It was four o'clock; and we were a thousand feet above the canyons. But the ridges were closer. Five, maybe seven hundred feet below. We came around for the final pass; and Cliff, kneeling beside Foster, had the mike in his hand and his goggled head thrust into the slipstream. He peered through the smoke, counting out seconds of drift correction, then said into the mike, "Cut!" Don throttled down the thundering engine (to make it easier for Chuck to plunge out through the prop-blast), and the wind moaned sadly around the door. Cliff slapped Foster on the shoulder, and out Chuck went with a war-whoop. <u>Gee, perfect body position</u>! <u>That's the way to do it</u>! We watched his chute crack open, and as the plane circled, we saw him float slowly down and land fifty feet from the burn. <u>Boy, what a jump</u>! <u>Beautiful</u>. <u>And so close to the fire he looked like he'd be in it there for awhile</u>.

We were coming around again, and Cummings and I moved down the bench and hooked our static lines to the cable over the door. Both of us would be going out this pass; so Cummings sat in the door, his feet out on the step, and I crouched behind him. Cliff checked everything a last time and told us to plane away from the fire as soon as we got open---advice resulting from Foster landing dangerously close to the burn.

We were set. The motor died. There was the slap. Bob shoved off and dropped away, and I threw myself out after him. The next thing I knew both chutes were open, and Cummings was level with me, swinging under his canopy a few yards away. I checked my canopy. No lines over. Then looked for the fire. There it was, down left. A tug on the guideline twirled me away from it. Now plane, haul the front risers down and keep 'em there. I felt the wind pick up as air spilling from the rear of the chute drove me forward at six, eight, ten miles an hour.

But whoa. I'm going too far. Cliff must have put us out farther from the fire than he did Chuck. When will I learn to make my own decisions about wind, and not take for gospel what the spotter says! So halfway down I turned around again to plane back. Never make it now, but I can still get a little closer.

Cummings didn't turn, kept going the other way, and sailed off to land half a mile from the fire. I came down a quarter-mile closer, but still a long way off. I hung limp in the risers; and a puff of wind slung me into the hill sideways. The stuff was all brush, with here and there a decent-sized tree; and I crashed down into the springy ten-foot tangle and folded at the hips around a wrist-thick branch. I was all set to feel injured when the branch gave under me, and I went on through and stopped a few feet from the ground.

I heard Foster yelling way up the mountain and finished sacking up my chutes and started slantwise up the slope toward him. The brush (which had made our landings soft) was exasperating now, as thick as any jungle and hampering every step. Foster had left his gear to set up the radio on the ridge and was talking to the plane about the best place to drop cargo. There was enough smoke to make things pretty vague to

those in the plane; and when our cargo came out
of the Noorduyn's belly, we watched the burlap
chute and its daisy-chain of firepacks disappear
into the edge of the burn. When we found them,
one pack was burning, ruining the clackboards and
loosening a flood of feathers from the charred end
of one sleeping bag. The tools were all right
though, the pulaskis (ax-adzes) and shovels. We
came out of the burn juggling hot canned goods
and cached everything beside the radio and went
to work. Nobody answered our shouts, and the
ground crew wasn't anywhere around.

About 5:30 the Noorduyn was back with
the second stick, and Fieldhouse, Speaker, and
Kaarhus burst out of the sky upon us. Six men.
Not enough against this big a fire---even if the
ground crew were here. It's a shame the Siskiyou
couldn't have spared twelve.

Nevertheless we kept on cutting fire-trail
along the ridge, the best place to halt the fire's
march; and it was slow hacking work through the
maddening brush. The ground crew showed up a
little later, six weary men and a crew-boss. They
had been eight miles down the trail toward home
(after leaving the little burn, as they thought,
mopped up and cold) when smoke churning up the
mountain behind them told the story. Somewhere
in that black eighth of an acre they had missed one
tiny spark (by not patrolling an extra twenty-four
hours as they should have), and the afternoon sun
had done the rest. So here was a many-fingered
monster eating away the mountain greenery, with
not enough men at hand to stop it. And this tired
ground crew had taken twice as long to come back

over eight rugged trail-miles as we had to be
summoned and travel 120 miles by air from
Oregon.

Then, surprise of surprises, a helicopter
came flap-flapping overhead, reconnoitering and
dropping supplies. Of course, California had said
over the phone they would try to get a helicopter
in to help us, but we thought they were just
talking. Before dark the 'copter even dropped a
man or two into deep brush farther up the ridge.
Dangerous business dropping men that way
without jump-suits. And we found ourselves,
smokejumpers, shuddering at the thought of
untrained men falling even fifteen feet into
branches and rocks without our padding and face-
guards and crotch protection.

So now we had fourteen men, and night
was falling. The fire wasn't moving so steadily
since the heat of the afternoon slacked off; so we
split into two crews clearing trail in opposite
directions around the burn. One crew took time
out to clear a helicopter landing---a thirty-foot level
square---on a shoulder of the ridge. We worked all
night, using headlamp flashlights from our
firepacks, and hoped to tie the fire in all around
before the sun warmed it up in the morning.

But the fire had already devoured twenty-
five acres, and dawn caught us far from ringing it
in. The helicopter made a couple of trips as soon
as it was light; but then fog moved in cutting off
all aerial contact. Fog. Thick white heavy stuff;
and wet. Bad for flying, but wonderful for keeping
fires quiet. We worked on till 3:30 in the afternoon, thankful for the break which prevented the

fire from roaring away before we could get it under
control. And finally we met the other crew. The
trail, running almost two miles through a torturous
never-ending mat of manzanita and deerbrush, was
finished.

We jumpers went back through the strange
white world of fog gathering our chutes and jump-
gear; and it started to rain. Foster, who had left
his stuff to set up the radio as soon as he landed,
found the fire had spread beyond his landing spot,
burning his whole outfit. Parachutes, suit, helmet-
-everything. It looked like Cliff had been right to
dump Cummings and me farther away. Foster's
rope was a coiled skeleton of ashes, and he came
back carrying all that remained of his equipment---
the fire-blackened rip-ring of his reserve.

The rain killed off the fire, but kept the
'copter away too. We were hoping for a ride out
the next day because we didn't want to repeat
Nolan's tedious struggle over to the trail. That
night we slept fitfully in the rain; and lightning
pelted into the ridges all around us. At last here
was the storm that had held the other jumpers up
in the Siskiyou---and held them, as we found out
later, needlessly. It was my luck to get the partly
burned sleeping bag, and all night I lay in a sodden
maelstrom of feathers, watching a white smudge
of moon creep interminably across the sky.

Monday morning was beautiful and clear,
with pools of fog lying in the valleys below us.
The helicopter came in about eight o'clock and
started shuttling us out. A wonderful sight, that
bright red craft leaping off the ridge-spur in the
sunlight. It made three trips first with gear---tools,

chutes, jump-suits, canteens, packs---and
everything soaked. Then ourselves, one at a time
(for a small 'copter can carry only 200 pounds
besides the pilot) in eighteen-minute round-trips to
a meadow a few miles away. That marvelous red
dragonfly accomplished in nine minutes apiece
what would have taken us twelve back-breaking
hours to do on foot---get ourselves out to a road.

I was third man out, on this, the second
time in history that smokejumpers have been taken
out of a fire by helicopter: Running in under the
madly flailing rotor, yelling to be heard above the
noise of the engine and slap-slapping blades; then
closing the door and seeing the grass flatten as the
engine at your back deafens you in take-off, and
the mountainside drops away through the plexiglas
at your feet. Exciting time.

As the funny little machine thrashed its way
up over the back ridge, Mount Shasta rose into
view, a great gleaming pyramid in fresh snow,
with gray clouds hiding its base. Coming just at
that moment, the noble mountain seemed a fitting
symbol of our escape from the weariness and filth
of firefighting into the civilized world of hot baths
and breakfasts and clean white sheets.

McCarthy Wises Up

I don't know why Red McCarthy ever came to a smokejumper camp in the first place. He thought he was so tough before he got here that he acted like the Forest Service was strictly made up of lilies. Of course, he'd been in the sub service during the war and had been a steeplejack and high steel worker back east; and we're as ready as the next gang to give credit where credit is due. But this guy McCarthy would <u>never</u> stop blowing about how tough he was and how much he knew and how any part of the world he hadn't seen wasn't worth seeing. He showed up pretty well in the training though, making the best slip-jump of anybody in camp but Dan Cahill, our foreman. And out of the seven practice jumps, McCarthy won the ten-dollar pot four times for coming closest to the mark with his steering slots. But the guy didn't have a friend in the world 'cause all he'd do is brag, brag, brag.

He first tangled with Big Jim Pierce when we were on the trail maintenance detail over on Ponyshoe Ridge. There hadn't been any fires for awhile, and there wasn't any lightning danger in the Siskiyou; so Dan decided the bottom five men on the jump list could be spared to make the overnight climb to Ponyshoe to clear a year's growth of brush and windfalls off the trail. Dan put Jim Pierce, a tall quiet guy who's been a smokejumper two summers now, in charge of us.

The truck took us up to where the trail cuts out of Meeker's Valley and we started---Johnson, Colter, MaCarthy, Jim and myself---up the rocky switchbacks that lead to the ridge. We had two packs---chow and sleeping bags---plus the cross-cut saw bowed in a teardrop on the lightest pack. The other three men carried the rest of the outfit: two brush hooks, a pulaski and a gallon canteen. We'd trade off, carrying the packs for awhile, then taking our turn with the tools. At first it was steep climbing but not much brush to cut; and we worked our way up above Meeker's Valley in a couple of hours. But then the trail got fainter, and the manzanita crowded right over it lots of places. Jim and I were on the brush hooks through there, and we hacked away till the blades got dull and wouldn't cut and our backs felt like they'd break from stooping over so long. The guys with the packs made much better time; and when we caught up with them at noon, they were sitting under a tree in the shade taking in the blue-and-white cone of Mount Shasta eighty miles away. Jim and I were stripped to the waist and sweating like race horses, and it didn't improve our spirits to see Red McCarthy finishing off one of the cans of peaches that was supposed to be dessert for supper tonight.

All Jim said was, "We share the chow on this trip, Red. Remember that tonight when the rest of us have peaches." Then he sheathed his brush hook and put on his shirt and began digging into his paper sack of sandwiches. "I know two guys who aren't gonna be hooking brush for awhile, too," he said. "Cocoa and me."

After lunch we filed a good edge on all the tools; and then Jim and me shouldered the packs and started on ahead, leaving McCarthy and Colter swinging the brush hooks and Johnson carrying the pulaski and canteen.

"You're in charge of the next patch of brush, Red," Jim yelled at McCarthy, who was bringing up the rear. "So get that trail clean." Then we started ahead with the packs and the saw.

It was a beautiful trail, for just walking along. Way on top of the world with jumbles of shaggy blue ridges fading away to the horizons on both sides, and Shasta tall and white ahead of us. We hadn't hit a big windfall all day, and even though the packs were heavy it was a good place to be. There were a few little knobby pine in the trail, that Johnson could take care of with the ax-blade of the pulaski; so we hiked right along. Jim's idea was to work about ten hours covering most of the trail the first day, so we could take it easy on the way down to Eight Dollar Ranch in the morning.

By two o'clock the brush was thinning out,

and we dipped into the timber again. A big white fir about four feet through was down across the trail at one spot; so Jim and I unlimbered the saw and got to work. We figured there was brush enough behind us to hold the other guys for a couple of hours yet and thought we'd have a section out of the log by the time they came along. The log was running straight downhill, and we had to be careful not to get the saw pinched for good as the log settled.

Boy, that Jim Pierce sure drags a smooth saw. We slid down through that fir like nobody's business, listening to the blade sing and feeling the easy rhythm in our shoulders. Johnson came up just as the saw began to bind, and we used the pulaski to wedge open the cut enough to finish it. We were oiling the saw-blade for the second cut when Colter and McCarthy strolled in. McCarthy was walking with his head tipped back and his elbows out, acting like he was king of the world.

Johnson and Colter spelled Jim and me on the saw while Red McCarthy sat down on the butt of the log to watch them work. Jim was wondering how they'd caught up with us so fast, and he walked back along the trail cussing like mad and chewing McCarthy out good.

"What the hell, Red! I thought I told you this morning that when we clear trail, we clear it wide enough for a man on a horse to get through. At least two feet---better three---of clearance all along, and no brush in the trail more than ankle high."

"Yep," said McCarthy, yawning.

"Well, damn your hide, I walked five minutes

back there and passed a dozen places where the brush touches across the trail. And here's the only thing that was cleared in that whole stretch." And he threw down a loped-off fir limb.

"Listen, Pierce," McCarthy said, "I didn't come out here to cut brush. I came here to parachute on fires, and if this stinkin' timber doesn't start burning pretty soon, I'm going back to hanging steel and make some real money."

"Okay, McCarthy. You'll probably be going back sooner than you think. But right now we've got this trail to clear. Colter, why the hell didn't you cut brush back there?"

"Well, you said Red was in charge, and he said as long as we could walk through okay it was clear enough."

"Yeah, and in another year that brush'll be so thick you won't be able to find a trail up here. Okay you lazy sonsabitches. This just means we work late today and put in eight hours tomorrow too." And he picked up Colter's brush hook and pointed back along the trail. "Let's go, McCarthy. Oh, no, after you; so I can watch you."

It was a wonder Jim didn't turn McCarthy in to Dan Cahill for goofing off that day. But I guess it was because Red worked like a fiend after that bawling out. Of course, the guy wasn't any more sincere about the job. He was just trying to show Pierce that he was the better man and could cut brush faster than anybody else around. Trying to pat himself on the back as usual. He and Jim kept up a terrific pace back along that three miles of brush, each trying not to be left behind by the other. When they came up to our supper fire, they

moved slow, all their strength drained away. And
they weren't talking at all.

Jim and the redhead didn't have any more
run-ins for quite a few weeks after that, but
everybody knew they weren't exactly buddies.
Most all the camp sided with Pierce, too, because
nobody could stand McCarthy's line of gaff very
long. Like on that phone line construction we did
over at Pistol River. He was always telling
everybody how to wind insulators and make ties
just like he was God himself. Red was pretty good
at it, and he loved to climb; but why he always
had to spout off and talk in a snarl to make people
think he was tough I don't know.

We were building a Forest Service line to
connect the ranger stations; and we strung wire
from tree to tree along the old Pistol River Road.
Some places there weren't trees enough, so we
cut poles and peeled them and set them up and
tied the wire in that way. McCarthy hogged the
climbers all day (even though his shins must have
got rubbed raw) just because a guy in belt and
climbing spurs, jingling with staples and all those
tools hanging in his belt, looks rugged. I'm telling
you that guy would do anything if it made him look
rugged. He was cocky about his climbing too,
always talking about how low these trees were
compared to the sky-scrapers he'd worked on. Of
course he stopped talking for an hour or two the
day he chickened out of climbing that big doug fir
with rotten bark. Jim had laid out the wire and
decided to string it on a long tie from the big tree
about forty feet from the ground to clear a bunch
of low oaks. But McCarthy refused to climb the

fir; said it was unsafe. So Jim came back to look
it over. It was a rough tree to climb all right; six
feet through and full of little stub branches to
catch a climbing cable on. The bark was rotten
almost all the way around, too. Jim looked around
to see if any other tree nearby would take the
wire, but the big fir stood all by itself on a slope
thick with young reproduction. It would take all
day to brush out a path for the wire using any
other tree. So he took the spurs and belt from
McCarthy and got ready to climb it himself. The
leather strap wasn't long enough to go around the
tree; so Jim rigged a cable into the snap-rings of
the belt and went up where the bark looked the
safest.

Well, it was a struggle all the way. Jim
Pierce tied that wire up there all right, but it took
him two hours to do it. Every time he moved a
spur on that tree he had to pound it in five or six
times before it would stay. And those little
branch-stubs stuck out just far enough so he
couldn't flip the cable over them without climbing
around the tree. He circled the tree twenty times
that way and was just about shot when he got
down. Like I say, McCarthy stopped talking about
himself for almost an hour after that.

One of the things that griped us most about
Red McCarthy though was the way he'd brag
about how drunk he'd get. And he didn't get
drunk at all. He'd just go up to the Hawk and
have a couple of beers and start staggering
around, pretending he was pie-eyed and talking
louder and tougher than usual. It was all a stupid
gag to impress us, and we got sick of it but quick.

One night Red came back to camp that way and wandered into our tent and really talked himself into a battle. Like I say Jim Pierce is a quiet guy, tall with dark hair; and he was sitting on his bunk oiling his boots when Loud-mouth McCarthy barged into the tent. The redhead was acting more soused than usual, really tottering around, and talking in a fake mushy whisper. Jim looked up and scowled but didn't say anything till McCarthy crossed toward him and stumbled and fell against the orange crate Jim used for shelves by his bunk. I think McCarthy was doing it just for effect, but he really smashed the crate. Jim's shaving stuff and his girl's picture clattered across the floor, and some change he had on the top shelf rolled down between the floorboards.

Jim stood up and yelled, "Get the hell out of this tent, McCarthy!"

McCarthy stuck his chin out and said in a thick voice, "Who's gonna make me?"

Jim lunged forward then, grabbed two big handfuls of Red's shirtfront, and ran him backwards out the tent door so fast he didn't know what hit him. Big Jim shoved him hard off the front step; and McCarthy sailed out and lit backwards on the cinders. When Red hit the ground, he sobered up fast. He came charging back into the tent snorting like a bull and his face so red I thought he'd pop. He drove into Jim Pierce like a buzz-saw; and they both went down, crashing against Jim's cot with the redhead on top. The cot caved in, and Jim's head cracked hard against the side-boards of the tent-frame. His neck seemed made of jello for a second, the way

he lolled his head around; and all the while Red
McCarthy was on top of him in a crazy fit of rage,
hammering punches into his face. I'd started
forward to drag the redhead off when Jim Pierce
came to life. He snapped his body over like a
falling cat, throwing McCarthy aside and getting
his hands and feet under him in one motion. While
he was still in a crouch, he threw a punch into
Mac's stomach that tied him in a little red knot.
Then Jim heaved himself to his feet, dragged the
redhead up by his shirt, and smashed him twice in
the face with that big right fist of his. McCarthy
was still hitting Jim in the chest and body, but his
blows got weaker each time Jim hit him. Pierce
was about to plaster him a third time when a big
shadow filled the doorway and Dan Cahill's voice
roared, "The next guy that swings can fight it out
with me!"

I guess it's partly because Dan Cahill has
shoulders like an ox and a couple of fists that are
known all the way to Missoula. And partly 'cause
he's got that commanding voice he picked up as
top-sergeant in the paratroops. But as much as
anything it's 'cause Dan is boss, foreman of this
jumper outfit, that Jim Pierce and Red McCarthy
cut short the roughhouse.

Not that Dan likes us kowtowing to his
authority. There's nothing a parachute-fireman
needs more than initiative once he's out the door
of that plane. But one thing Dan won't stand for
is fighting in camp. Because when two or three
guys are dropped on a fire a hundred miles back in
the wilderness, they've got to work together or
they'll never get out alive.

Dan told them he'd can them both if either of them raised a hand again, and he told them to shake hands. McCarthy and Jim were both cut up; and they stood there, breathing hard and glaring at each other.

"Come on you two. Shake hands like a couple of men. Your gonna have to be friends out on that fireline."

McCarthy's eyes were bitter and twitching as he looked at Dan and then at Pierce. "I don't have to be friends with no man!" he said. And he spat on the floor and stalked out.

Things didn't improve between Jim and Red the next few days either. Dan put them on different work-details to keep the peace, but you could tell the way they looked at each other in the mess hall it wouldn't take much to set them off again. The next week that airliner crashed on the South Sister, and fourteen guys went in on a rescue jump. They needed lots of stretcher-bearers in there fast to take out the injured; and those boys really earned their overtime that day. Sixteen hours straight of carrying loaded stretchers over steep rocky trails to the nearest road. And then they had to go back and get their chutes.

That put the rest of us up near the top of the jump list, and we began itching to hear that phone ring. I was number one on the list then and McCarthy two with Johnson, Peters and Kolchek next. I knew a fire-jump with McCarthy would mean I'd have to listen to him talk for maybe a week, till we packed out; but I was anxious to get going anyway. Like Mac said, we'd come out here to jump on fires; and our make-work jobs between times were beginning to get boring.

Sure enough that Saturday a big thunderstorm moved down the Cascades and belted lightning into a thousand ridges. The thunder rolled down the canyons, and Bill Peters said, "Ha, listen to that old cash register ring, boy. We're gonna be jumping soon."

By Sunday afternoon the lookouts had spotted dozens of new smokes and had started the suppression crews on their way. But back in the high country where there aren't any roads and the trails peter out, and where some of the sections haven't even been surveyed yet, you can't get in at all except by air. So we smokejumpers had a field day.

The first call came in Sunday at two o'clock, for three men on a lightning strike ten miles south of Pyramid Mountain. That meant me, McCarthy and Johnson---if Dan went according to the jump list. Dan thought it over, the fact that we were all first year jumpers, and had just about decided to send us when there was a crash against the wall of the hangar. It was Jim Pierce laying into Red McCarthy again because the redhead had gone by with his jump-gear on his shoulder and smirked, "Don't you wish you were going on a firejump, Jimmy-baby? Cry, Jimmy-baby; cry!"

Dan tore out of the hangar and lunged between them and held them apart. He shook his head disgustedly and then let them go; and his voice was cold when he said, "Johnson, you stay here. Pierce is jumping in your place this time. We should have one experienced man in there with Cocoa and Red." That's what he said, but you

could see that wasn't why he was putting
McCarthy and Pierce together on a jump. They'd
settle this thing for good one way or the other
before they came back.

"Now get that plane loaded and get into
your gear!" Dan yelled as Jake Oldfield, our pilot,
kicked the engine over.

The next minute Jim and McCarthy and I
were dumping our sacks of jump-gear out on the
concrete and were pulling on our canvas suits and
football helmets and quick-release harnesses. The
rest of the guys were loading the plane with burlap
cargo chutes and the firepacks that held our
canteens, rations, sleeping bags, and fire tools. I
stuffed the climbing spurs, fannol saw and rope on
top of the signal streamers in my baggy leg-
pocket, and Jim carried the radio in with his rope.

Dan came out with two maps of where the
fire was and gave one to Jim and kept one himself.
Then he got into his spotter's chute and his helmet
and goggles while the squadleaders lifted our
chutes out of gray chafing bags and snapped them
into our harnesses. Jake had the engine
thundering as Bailey checked my main chute, my
reserve, the sheath-knife on top of the reserve,
and the safety catch on my quick-release plate.
Then he handed me my static line over my
shoulder, and I waddled forward to the plane.
Those jump outfits weigh close to seventy pounds
with the rope and all, and they're not easy to run
around in.

Dan had McCarthy already climbing into the
plane and wanted me to go in next. I guess he
wanted me to sit between Red and Jim Pierce in

case they felt mad enough at each other to be
cutting break cords or static lines or something.
Then Jim climbed in and sat on the end of the
bench that runs along the plane's port side. The
plane is a single-engined Norseman, six-place job---
big enough for most smokejumper situations. Dan
clambered over the firepacks to the co-pilot's seat,
and Jake taxied to the end of the runway and took
off.

The hole where the door had been taken out
looked big and easy to fall out of, and I tried to
keep my mind on the trees flashing by below so I
wouldn't be thinking about burning into the ground
if something went wrong with my chute. You've
got two of them, dope, and they'll both open; so
stop worrying. No matter how many jumps you've
made, you always sweat out each one for awhile
anyway. I'd been too busy on the ground to worry
much, but now I had time to think; and the
butterflies were starting to flop around in my
stomach. Then I got my mind on the cross-cut
saw piled on the firepacks in front of me, and I
was all right. The saw was bowed in a loop with a
guard over the teeth and two cans of oil lashed to
the handles. It had a driftchute tied to it, more to
mark where it would be dropped than to break its
fall. Every time the plane hit bumpy air the saw
kept nudging me in the knee, and finally I shoved it
back and hooked it over a shovel-handle to keep it
out of the way. Then I noticed Jim buckling the
facemask of his helmet and putting on his gloves,
so I did the same.

In twenty minutes we were over the fire,
and Dan was back beside us getting ready to spot

us in. Jake circled twice while Dan threw
driftchutes into the slipstream and we craned our
necks to get the lay of the land. It was rough
country, straight up and down, with thick timber
and no open spots. The fire, about half an acre
and burning uphill in a steady wind, was on the
spur of a big jagged butte.

Dan put us out beautifully, Jim on the first
pass, and me and McCarthy on the second. My
opening shock flipped the fannol saw out of my
leg-pocket (which I hadn't tied shut tight enough),
but I didn't miss it till we got down. Jim
disappeared into the trees about fifty yards from
the fire on the downhill side; and McCarthy and I
came down so close together I thought he was
going to walk on my canopy for awhile. We were
yelling back and forth and planing toward the fire
when all of a sudden the trees were up around us
and we were bouncing thumpity-thump down
through the branches. My canopy slipped through
the limbs for a while, and I thought it was going to
collapse and drop me like a rock; but finally it
caught and brought me to a springy stop about
thirty feet from the ground. The trees were tall,
doug fir mostly, with a few yellow pine---all big
mature timber that had never been burnt over.

It was funny, one minute being up in the
sunshine and the next being down in the shadowy
forest, everything looking like a big church. There
wasn't a sound for a second or two; then I heard
McCarthy cussing and saw him way up in a tall fir,
hung up for sure. He must have been a hundred
feet in the air easy, and he was out where he
couldn't get in to the trunk.

I laughed up at him, which only made him swear louder, then pulled my rope out of the leg-pocket to make my let-down. That's when I noticed the little jack-knife saw that went with the climbing kit was gone. I threaded the rope through my back pack belt, tied the three half-hitches to the risers, cracked my quick-release, and went down the rope with no strain. Then I heard Jim yelling from off in the woods, and he followed my shouts till he found us. He was out of his jump gear except for the canvas jacket, and he had the radio in his hand.

"The fire's about a hundred yards upslope," he said. "Not too big yet, if we get hot. Dan says the cargo will be coming down on the next pass; so look sharp for it."

We heard the plane diving and saw the cargo chutes snap open and sail down. The cross-cut saw with its driftchute fluttering landed pretty far away; but the daisy chain of firepacks crashed down through the trees and landed almost at our feet. That was a lucky break, 'cause lots of times you have to hunt a couple of hours for your cargo before you can do a darn thing.

McCarthy was still working on his letdown and was triple-checking every bend in his rope before he wanted to slide out of that nice safe harness. It's funny how careful you get when your life depends on getting a rope through certain D-rings and around your legs and body just right. I went off to bring back the saw while Jim broke out the pulaskis and shovels from the two firepacks, and Red McCarthy sweated it out high in the air. I could hear the fire then, crackling quietly in the undergrowth as it spread along the slope under the trees.

When I got back with the saw, Red was ready to take the plunge; so we watched while he held two thicknesses of the rope in his left hand, clouted the quick-release plate with his right, and eased out of his harness, braking the line through his gloves. He came down all right for twenty feet, then something caught and the rope wouldn't slide any more. The D-rings of his belt drew together, choking him at the waist with the force of his own weight. He squawked and went stiff and squirmed like a speared fish, but every move he made cinched the belt tighter around him.

"It's cutting me in two, guys," he grunted through clamped jaws. "Help. Help!" And his hands were desperately tracing the course of the rope to find where it had fouled.

"The climbers, quick! Where are the climbers?" yelled Jim. "Right here," I said, diving for the pocket in my jump suit.

Jim was strapping on the climbing spurs like a madman while I yanked my backpack belt out of the chute-board and rigged a piece of rope through it as climbing cable.

"You got the saw?" he asked, flinging the rope around the tree and fighting a cat's paw into the other ring.

"No, it fell out on my opening."

"Well, gimme a pulaski then, quick!"

I handed him one and he started up the tree like a topper, clawing his spurs into the bark and flipping the rope up rhythmically. McCarthy had stopped squirming and was just gurgling and

twirling slowly under his tight-stretched chain of
canopy, risers and rope. It was like seeing a guy
on a gallows, and all I could do from the ground
was send ripples up the rope hoping they would
start him sliding again. It was a good thing in a
way that his sheath-knife was up on his reserve
twenty feet above him, or he'd sure as hell have
cut himself loose and dropped. And he was still
eighty feet from the ground.

Even from where I was I could see his face
getting purple under that red hair, and I was
hopping up and down trying to help Jim climb
faster. The pulaski made things awkward, and he
almost dropped it when he stopped to tighten the
rope to fit the tapering diameter of the tree. A
pulaski is a big tool, an ax with an adze-head on
the back of the blade; and it's no hand-tool to use
in a tree. But it's the only thing we had since I'd
lost the fannol saw, and it had to do.

Jim hit the limbs at fifty feet, and from there
on up was solid branches all the way to the top.
The first ones were all dead, and he could knock
them off with one blow. But higher up they were
alive, and the going was tougher. Swinging a
pulaski over your head with both hands is rough
work, especially when one little slip can put it
through your foot or topple it out of your hands or
sink it through the rope that's holding you to the
tree. And being in such a god-awful hurry to get
McCarthy loose, Big Jim was really panting.

He drove his way up, blasting limbs loose,
skitting around the tree like a cat to get all the
branches, and climbing almost out of the loop
before he'd haul close to flip it up again. Man, I've

never seen such climbing! Every second or two a
branch would drift down lazily to crash in front of
me, and chips were drumming into the underbrush
like rain. He got level with McCarthy and eeled
out on a branch as far as he could. The redhead
was limp as a sack then, and we didn't know if he
was dead or not. I swung him in toward the tree
with the rope, and Jim stuck the pulaski out at
arm's length trying to hook the rope with the adze-
head. God, his arm was shaking! I don't see how
he held the pulaski in one hand at all after
chopping up all that way.

It was a lousy set-up because I couldn't pull
too hard on the rope for fear of ripping Red's
canopy loose from the tree above him. And yet I
had to get him over where Jim could reach him if
we were going to get him at all. Jim finally undid
his climbing rope, wiggled out on the branch till it
bowed way down, and hooked the pulaski on a
wave I sent running up the rope. Then he crawled
back, pulled the rope up into his hands, and tied
himself back into the climbing cable. He hauled
Red in to him, propped him on a branch, and
wrenched loose the killing tangle that was clamped
on his gut. Jim felt under his jump jacket and
yelled down that his heart was still beating, though
weak as hell. And he found that one of the snaps
on McCarthy's jump pants had fouled with the
rope where it wound around his leg. That had
kept him from sliding and made the belt cinch up
that way.

In five minutes the purple was out of
McCarthy's face, and he began coming around. At
first all he did was groan and make weak passes at

his stomach, like the belt was still there. But in a little while he was right awake, though he still couldn't talk much. Jim asked him if he felt up to climbing down yet, but he said he wanted to rest a while more. And he said, "Thanks a lot for getting me in time, Jim. I'm sorry I've been such a kid around camp lately."

"That's okay, Red. I guess we both acted like fools."

And they shook hands eighty feet in the air.

Being already up there, Jim went on up and cut the chute down; and Red tied the rope to a branch and came down in good style. Then Jim dropped the rope and chute and yelled, "Get hot on that fire, you guys, before this whole mountain burns down. I'll be with you in a minute." Then he screamed, "Bombs away!" and threw down the pulaski in a long end-over-end toss and started down the tree.

We worked till dark, digging firetrail and falling snags, and then broke out our headlamps and worked on while the cool of the night held the fire down. It was at about two-and-a-half acres--- and then we sat around and watched the embers wink out one by one in the cold of early morning.

It was a break that the fire hadn't crowned but just burned the brush along the ground. Most of the big trees even in the burn weren't killed, except the one the original lightning-bolt had split from top to bottom. We had the fire pretty well mopped up by Monday noon; and when we went over the burn by hand that evening, it was stone cold. Then we had twenty-four hours of sack-out patrol, just in case there was a spark we'd missed.

It's funny the way Red acted after that. I'd expected him to talk my arm off. But all during the fire and the two days it took us to pack out---in fact from the time he got out of that tree with a red welt around his stomach till we came swinging down the trail into Happy Flat---he worked like an anthill and didn't say a word about himself.

And you know who are the biggest buddies shooting pool up at the Hawk these days, don't you? Red McCarthy and Big Jim Pierce.

Summer Search, 1949

February call from Oberlin, Ohio:

"Hi Starr. How's it going, bro?"

"Hello Hughie! Fine with me. How about you?"

"Good if you like winter. Where you going to apply for work this summer?"

"Oh, Cave Junction, Oregon, again of course. And a couple of the other smokejumper bases too. Missoula, Montana---the big one. And maybe McCall, Idaho, and Winthrop, Washington."

"Gee, I'd like to get on as a smokejumper. Can you send me those addresses---and any others you know of---right away?"

"Sure thing."

"You think Cave Junction won't take you back? Or do you just want to try another outfit?"

"Well I was far from being your all-star smokejumper. I gave our foreman, Cliff Marshall, nothing but trouble. Almost derailed his training

schedule by getting my chin sliced in half on that
first jump. Then we had a fire right there in town
when a sawmill burned. Three of us got in a two-
hour waterfight with 6-gallon backpump cans on
that one. Those buggers shoot a stream for thirty
feet."

    "Oh. A little on the job R & R."

    "Yeah. But it was only after the fire was all
knocked down. But it sure put my butt in a sling."

    "You have a habit of doing that, don't you
Starr."

    "Well, I guess so. And then there was my
taking a camera along on all my jumps. But it
wasn't much of a fire season. Only got in one fire
jump---on a blaze down in California below Mount
Shasta. And then I got sick the last week of the
season---and had to go back in to that Grants Pass
hospital and have them take out my appendix.
Cliff let me lie around camp for 5 more days till I
was ready to take the bus home."

    "Wow."

    "And then, obnoxious sonofabitch that I am,
I had to argue with Cliff over some little gripe on
the last day on the job---thus proving to be entirely
ungrateful for all that he'd done for me."

    "Aw. Too bad."

    "I'm afraid Cliff Marshall would be out of his
gourd to hire me again this summer."

    "Well, that's too bad. But what should I
stress on my applications?"

    "All your fire experience. And tools you
know how to handle. Three different Forest
Service jobs with clear specifics as to where you
worked and what you did. Names and titles of

supervisors. Anything else that shows your
quality, brains, and staying power. Make that
muscles as well as staying power. They might not
go for brains."

"Okay, guy. Thanks. I'll do 'er."

"Go to it, Hugh. And good luck. I'll mail
you those addresses today."

So to my February's application in '49 Cliff
Marshall understandably says, "No thanks." All
the other smokejumper bases have the same
answer. They have the same answer for my
younger brother Hugh, about to turn twenty, who
already has three summers of Forest Service
laborer experience to draw on, and probably as
many fires as I have. And I'm sure that Hugh,
being wise as well as smart, has never sassed his
boss in the last week of employment.

So about June 8th we both are dejectedly
looking for some more mundane summer jobs, here
in our desert home town of Albuquerque, New
Mexico. Selling shoes perhaps? I am lucky to get
a lifeguard job at the lagoon in Tingley Park. And
Hugh is about to head out to California to try to
find more blister-rust work in the high country
when on June 15th the telegram comes.

Echoing in June:

Oh, I'm going to enjoy this. "Hey, Starr!
Look, I got a telegram! The Forest Service in
Missoula, Montana, wants me to come up there
and be a smokejumper if I can get there by June
20th!"

"Oh man! Wonderful! You can get there!

That's five days! Great, Hugh! That is great!"
And why didn't they take me? I'm the one with
smokejumper experience!

"They want me to let them know by return
telegram!"

"Well get right down there and send that
wire. Oh, that's great, Hugh. And you have
earned every bit of it."

But why wouldn't they take me? I'm the
one with nine jumps and seven fires and one
helicopter ride out! Son of a bitch!

So Hugh Jerome Jenkins, twenty years old,
honor student his freshman year at University of
New Mexico, now a junior at Oberlin College in
Ohio, home for the summer and seeking summer
work, has found it. And found it with the biggest
camp of the most elect of Forest Service hotshot
crews, the smokejumpers. The guys who
parachute out on fires, two at a time, to slay the
fire dragon not so far below. And save the forest.
And work like hell. And get paid good money to
do it!

A quiet, plain, slender guy, Hugh. Never a
big socialite; never a remarkable athlete; but a hard
worker with a sense of humor---and a man who
reads and thinks. The little brother I haven't seen
much of since going off to college myself in '42,
and then military service in '43---and seen less of
since he went away to Oberlin after I got back to
New Mexico. But now he has done it, and he's
earned that position with all his good woods
experience since '46. Congratulations, Hugh!

But why couldn't they have taken me too?
In a day Hugh has sent his telegram,

gathered up work shirts, work pants, boots, hat, jacket, sox, skivvies and duffelbag, and whatever cash he can lay his hands on and has hit the road, hitch-hiking the 1200 or so miles to Missoula, Montana. [You really can't get there from here.] And I have begun to figure out how and why this disaster has happened.

It must be, in the Missoula smokejumper base, that a very few of the guys accepted in March have not shown up for work on their June 15th reporting date for employment. So the chief foreman, finding a few no-shows on his roster, has sent out telegrams to the next experienced guys in line on the selected-application list. Some of these guys like Hugh are now jumping at the chance to be smokejumpers at last. But others are now already settled into other summer jobs---maybe at higher pay---or summer plans, or European vacations, or marriages, or whatever. So some of those return telegrams will not come---or will likely say, "No. Thanks a lot but no thanks."

So, anticipating this, what if I send in a telegram right now, outlining my experience one more time: "Cave Junction smokejumper last year, 9 jumps, plus a previous heavy fire season in California with the Forest Service. 7 fires total; veteran; distance runner, etc. Can be there by June 20."---? Just maybe they will have one hole left.

And it works. A telegram comes back saying simply, "You're hired. Come on up."

So a day later, filled with joy and exuberance, I hit the road, hitch-hiking on the trail of my kid brother Hugh---who was hired first remember---on the 1200-mile road to Missoula, Montana.

My last ride is a breathtaking careen in a big red Cadillac with a hardware salesman, over the Continental Divide from Helena at 85 miles per hour.

As I walk, still trembling, into the Federal Building in Missoula and find the right Forest Service office, the young woman sitting at the desk gives me a startled look. "You must be Starr," she says.

"That's right. How did you know?"

"Your brother, Hugh, just came through here an hour ago, and you look sort of like him."

"And did you tell him I also got hired?"

"Yeah."

"Aw shucks. I wanted to surprise him."

"He was mighty surprised." She sits there grinning at me. "I sort of like that. The young one hired first. The old boy, who knows it all, hired last. I think that's kinda neat."

Region One's Sixteen National Forests in 1949

In Montana

      The Beaverhead
      The Custer
      The Deerlodge
      The Flathead
      The Gallatin
      The Helena
      The Kootenai
      The Lewis and Clark
      The Lolo

In Idaho

      The Bitterroot (partly in Montana)
      The Clearwater
      The Coeur d'Alene
      The Kaniksu (partly in Washington)
      The Nezperce
      The St. Joe

In Washington

      The Colville

First Jump, Region One

Ninemile Airstrip, Smokejumper Training Camp; 35 miles northwest of Missoula, Montana; a sunny morning late in June:

The unpaved airstrip has been bladed out of the rolling green forest, and this humorous old plane flown over from Missoula a bit after 8 every morning. The dew is still on the grass.

As the first Ford Trimotor load of first-time jumpers rumbles away for takeoff, the smokejumper training foreman glances at his clipboard. He looks around at the tense young men nervously putting on their jump suits and chute harnesses for their very first parachute jump, and his usually booming voice moderates a bit. "Let's see. <u>Hugh</u> Jenkins! I want to see <u>Hugh</u> Jenkins. Come over here a minute, will you?"

"Sure," says the quiet half-suited jumper with the dark crew-cut. "What can I do for you, Fred?"

Fred takes Hugh aside a little from the rest of the men, as Hugh fidgets with the helmet in his hand.

"Now Hugh, you and your brother are both in the next plane-load. Four sticks; two men to a stick. You for your first jump ever, and he for his first refresher jump this year. Do you want to jump together?"

"Hey, that would be nice. Yeah, I'd like that."

"Okay. Now, do you want to go first of the pair? We hired you first, you know."

"Well that's okay with me, if that's what you want. But maybe you better let him go first. Experienced man and all that."

"You're sure?"

"Yeah. It might put him in a funk for the whole summer to have to go second to me."

The foreman's tough face crinkles in a grin. "Okay, Hugh. You're the kind of brother us ego-types need. You'll be second man in the third stick. He'll be first."

"Thanks, Fred." Hugh starts away.

"And Hugh," Fred says. "Let's have this be confidential between us."

"Right Boss," says Hugh. "And thanks for giving me those chances."

After a bit more conversation with two other men, the foreman scribbles again on his clipboard. He shouts at the men. "Okay! Navon! Harpole! DeJarnette! Tripp! Followed by Jenkins-Starr and Jenkins-Hugh! Followed by Linton-Jerry and Linton-Rob!"

"Hey, that's two sets of brothers in one flight!"

"Right. And don't forget you're all brothers

when you go out that door."

"Hey, that's right. Brothers in the sky."

"And don't forget another thing: We will spot you to the best of our ability. But if the wind shifts---even 180 degrees---between our drift chute and when you step out, you've got to figure that out in your first ten seconds after your chute opens. So look up first and check your chute for line-overs. Then look down at your boots and see how they are drifting over the terrain below. Then find your target-spot and drive that chute there."

"Right Boss."

"And don't worry. That chute _will_ open. Okay. The men I just called; suit up! The spotters will put your chutes on and check you out. And then you will check each other out, and wait for the order to climb aboard."

The trimotor lifts off with its usual loud alacrity and climbs nimbly into the sunny sky. Inside, four jumpers are sitting all suited up on the bench along the plane's left side, and the rest of us are milling about forward trying not to get our chutes tangled on any of the plane's equipment or each other while the spotter, Chuck Pickard, is forward farther still with the pilot.

We have an extra spotter along to simulate the assistant who helps the spotter drop cargo after the jumps on a typical fire. But there are no firepacks or tools aboard this trip, so there is plenty of room to move about. Out the windows the mountain ranges of western Montana are rugged in many directions, ridge upon ridge upon ridge; and the air is cool and still moist with dew fuming off the trees below. None of us think about not having seatbelts on, even the men who have flown into Missoula two weeks before on Northwest Airlines from Chicago. Because seatbelts are not yet in cars in 1949, and we're going to jump out of this plane anyway; so who the hell needs a seatbelt?

But it's easy to see that, under our bravado, some of these guys [all?] are really sweating it out. I look at Hugh and wave my static-line snap at him with a gloved thumbs-up and make my left hand into a slowly descending chute of curved fingers. He grins in reply behind his facemask and puts his arms over his reserve chute in a step-out stance and nods affirmative. So I think we'll both be okay.

The roar of the Ford's three uncowled engines tears in through the plane's sides and the doorless door and even through some open windows on this ancient aircraft; and the clattering metallic sound crashes through the ear-holes of our football helmets that most of us have buckled on by now. And I check that neither Hugh nor I have a chinstrap on our helmets and that both of our big collars are all the way up.

Chuck Pickard is spotting this group and is wearing a flatpack and harness and a gray leather spotter's cap now so his goggles can come down over his eyes when needed.

As we drone to 1500 feet he moves back among us, lowers those goggles, gets to the door and flings a softball-sized drift chute toward the red X on the timber-patched meadow below. After it opens, he follows it for a long time as it moves

among the treetops. He sees it land and offsets
that amount of drift, makes a mental mark on the
ground where his first pair of jumpers will step out.
Then he yells, "Navon and Harpole! Hook up!"

Two sticks later, when it's our turn, I nudge
Hugh and slide to the aft end of the bench and he
slides down next to me again.

Chuck Pickard, eyes twinkling, yells at us,
"Jenkins and Jenkins!" We stand up in that
strange pulled-over stance that smokejumpers in
gear must assume. He's pointing at me; "You're
Starr?" I nod. "And you're Hugh?" Hugh nods
also. "Okay, Jenkins brothers. Hook up!"

We snap our metal clasps into the cable and
slide them right, and Pickard checks us over
carefully. He nods that I am now okay, and I slide
forward to the half-kneel, left foot out on the little
step below the door, gloved hands gripping both
sides of the roaring oval door.

Pickard yells, "Okay, Brother Starr; do it
right for ol' Cave Junction. When you hear the
engines die, wait for the slap. Then go out
straight and happy, you lucky son of a bitch!"

He turns to Hugh. "And Brother Hugh.
When he gets out that door, you step right up
there and pop right after him and I won't give you
no slap at all. You got it?"

"Got it!" says Hugh.

I can sense Hughie crouching behind me, all
hooked up and sweating but ready to move out as
soon as I get out of the way. Pickard feels the
plane banking into the right path. He's got his
goggled head out the open window of this old
streetcar and has his left hand in a simulated plane

shape for signaling the pilot. The pilot, Slim Phillips, is flying the plane with his head turned back, eyes glued to Pickard's signal hand. When the hand quits flying and cuts like a cleaver, Slim pulls his throttles back, tilts the plane into a glide, and the clattering roar becomes barely a herd of crickets.

I'm pretending to study Squaw Peak and the Flathead Indian country to the north when SLAM comes Pickard's gentle slap on my shoulder. I step off straight and easy, elated to be back in the smokejumper business, with my classy kid brother Hugh---who was hired first remember---leaping out the door right behind me.

That first straight step slides into a slow rotation right, and by the time the chute blams open I am in a head-down dive, snapped back into a heads-up pendulum swinging wildly through almost 330 degrees before she settles into mere giant swings in the rocking slipstream. Hugh has opened above me and to my left in a much more stable manner, and we both are yelling with joy and the fact that we are open and walking on air and not too close together and other numerous blessings of sunlight through silk.

It is a great day above Camp Ninemile, Montana; a moment we will never forget. Being alive and happy and on our own way down to the lovely tree-bristling Earth, and being at the beginning of a fire season in the vast Northern Region in the greatest fire crew in the world. And being brothers in the sky.

Letters from a Smokejumper
(Hugh)

Camp Ninemile, USFS, Huson, Montana
July 2, 1949

Dear Charles,

Believe it or not, here I am learning to be a smokejumper. I was turned down all three places I applied for the job, was looking around Albuquerque for whatever work was available (damn little), and was about to head out to California for the old blister-rust job, when on June 15th I got a telegram from the Forest Service office in Missoula offering me employment as a smokejumper if I could get up here by June 20th. My brother Starr got an offer at about the same time, and we're up here together. So far everything looks pretty terrific; interesting (if strenuous) work, lovely country, a bizarre group of fellow employees, ideal chow, and $1.43 an hour, which to me looks like a lot of money.

We've been in training since we got here
(our camp is 30-odd miles northwest of Missoula),
and so far we have made three jumps, with four
more coming up next week. The first week was
all ground training. We'd spend each morning on
"units"---one hour at calisthenics, tumbling and
running the obstacle course; one hour on the
"shock tower" (in which we jump, dressed in our
cumbersome suits and harness, from a fifteen-foot
tower, with a rope jerking us to a halt before we
hit); one hour on the "mock ups" (in which we
practice correct position, etc.); and one hour of
rope let-downs in which we learn to let ourselves
down out of trees we may hang up in. Afternoons
are spent either in learning first aid, fire-
suppression, radio operation, etc., or "project
work"---chopping and sawing logs. It's a pretty
tough pace, but there are enough ordinary guys
like me sprinkled in among the hot-rocks to make it
tolerable.

Jumping, although completely safe, is quite
a novel and exhilarating sport. It's also been the
easiest part of the job, since on the mornings we
do it we spend most of the time just sitting around
watching the other fellows come in. I've made
good, easy landings every time, although when
swinging on the rope during ground training I
couldn't roll worth a damn. As an added interest,
an employee of Henry Luce, named Peter
Stackpole, has been snooping around taking
hundreds of pictures of the outfit with an
assortment of cameras. He says he's hoping for a
l4-page spread on the Forest Service in some
future issue of LIFE, of which a portion will be

devoted to smokejumpers. Could be. Fourteen pages seems to be a lot of attention for such a pillar of capitalism to give to a government agency. Maybe it's an expose' of communist infiltration. Lots of fellows here wear bright red woodsmen's hats.

I hope you are looking forward to Yale with more eagerness than I am to another frustrating year at Oberlin. Lately I've been considering Oberlin as a necessary evil---something you have to make yourself stand, like a cold shower. After all, it's only a year. Still, a year spent under the intellectual dictatorship of the Sage of South Professor is not one to invite anticipation. I don't know what I'd do without my annual summer tonic of a stretch with the Forest Service. The paradox is that, in spite of my discomfort at Oberlin, an academic career is the only really attractive one for me. Thanks again for the notes you gave me. I've been reading them, and the occasional illegible word only makes me concentrate more. Well, my regards and good wishes. Write sometime.

Sincerely,

Hugh

Camp Ninemile, USFS, Huson, Montana
July 5, l949

Dear Folks,

Well, we're all back at work again after a long Fourth of July weekend. And appropriately today we had our fourth jump, out of a big old C-47---also called a DC-3 or a Doug---a twin-engined plane of the thirties and early forties. We had a longer wait in the plane this time, since we loaded up at the airfield in Missoula and flew out here to jump near camp. It was okay, although my chute opened inside out and the lines were consequently so fouled together that I couldn't guide it, and I drifted down about two hundred yards wide of the mark I was supposed to hit. They say that happens occasionally (one of the fellows that jumped in Washington had the same thing occur), but it is of no importance as far as speed of descent goes. These chutes are about the most reliable things in the world, and having a reserve makes the whole thing about as safe as anything can be. It is still very exciting, of course, each succeeding jump the more so.

Was glad to hear that you got the record-player fixed and hope you've gotten around to listening to the Brahms, which I think is the best of the lot. You don't need a new needle. That's a new one and it should last several months . . . .

This afternoon we received training in retrieving cargo chutes. A few were dropped in the trees, and we went in with climbers and belt-cables to climb the trees to get them down. We were finished in an hour or so and spent the rest of the afternoon just lying around. Very nice.

Love,
Hugh

Memory From a Letter Lost

Jump #6, early July;
From a Trimotor Ford, over Ninemile Strip:

As Hugh Jenkins and another man leaped out, both parachutes opened well, but by some vagary of wind or body-swing they found themselves too close together.

Midair collision! With the second, higher, man's boots and suit and reserve chute getting tangled in Hugh's suspension lines above his head.

A hair-raising and dangerous situation, since the upper chute can collapse in a moment if properly blanketed by the lower. And the two chutes tangled together can cause both to tilt and circle each other and come down faster, with the upper man likely to smash the lower. And with lines and men tangled, deployment of either reserve chute may be not only useless but may only increase the tangle and the blanketing effect.

Hugh did the only effective thing. He seized the emergency knife from his chestpack sheath and "cut just the right lines" to free both parties.

After both men swung free and came down without injury, Hugh wrote that he was "a hero around there for about five minutes."

Flight to the Kaniksu

After the three weeks of training and the
seven practice jumps, the seventy new men were
considered qualified for their jobs. (The one old
retread from Region Six, being considered not quite
a true-blue Missoula-quality jumper, was given four
refresher jumps rather than the customary two
required for returning Missoula jumpers. This
discrimination on R-I's part was quite under-
standable to me and quite enjoyable. I would
much rather have four practice jumps than just
two.)

The last of the seven jumps for the new
men was the "graduation jump," on a real forest
fire set as an exercise by Lolo National Forest
rangers out on Hayes Creek, a few miles southwest of Missoula. I got to go along on that one,
leaping out of a Doug with eighteen other guys in
four-man sticks. The first man in each stick gets
to stand in that curving open door and, because of
the bulge of the plane's side, he can, if he wants

to, stick his helmeted head up into that roaring 90 mile-per-hour slipstream for a blast of fresh air. I wanted to.

Peter Stackpole of LIFE was out photo-graphing some of this from the air and some from the ground as we came sailing in. In spite of the smoke and flame, after getting down out of our trees, getting out of our gear and sacking it up, the first order of business was, incredibly, lunch. Someone had gone to considerable trouble to set up an entire splendid hot-food field cafeteria for us---and for all the visiting Forest Service brass who were inspecting this operation---out on the creekside just below the briskly crackling flames. As we lounged in the 70-man chow-line and filled our plates then our faces, and burped through a brief siesta in order to let the fire get big enough to be a real challenge, camp comedian smokejumper Jack Rose of Los Angeles entertained us with endless John-Belushi-like routines. ["I ain't here like the rest of you ruff-<u>fiends</u>. I'm here gadderin' material for a novel!"] When we finally got to work about 1 PM, the fire was so big it almost got away from us and took all weekend to corral and put out.

When all the new men were qualified about a week into July, it was time to send them and the others out on project. Region One can't afford to keep 150 parachute-firemen hanging around the firehouse polishing the brass because there isn't that much work around the firehouse, and the rest of the Region's national forests are where there is plenty of work needing to be done. So after holding a reserve of 30 around the firehouse, the bosses assign the rest of the men sometimes singly, sometimes in two's, fours, eights or dozens, to all kinds of labor jobs out on the forests until the fires start to pop.

Dave Navon, for example, forestry graduate of the University of California, Berkeley, was sent to Seeley Lake, Montana, to help the district ranger on real timber cruising chores. Doing them one day, he was charged by a rutting bull moose, with no damage to moose or man.

At the other end of the scale, thirteen of us were loaded into a Doug with our baggage (but no jump suits) to fly some 200 miles northwest of Missoula to our project in the Kaniksu National Forest. Among us we had Tom "Jock" Hendrickson, a young married rodeo cowboy (whenever he could afford to participate in that arduous profession). Jock was a picturesque, humorous dark French-looking Montanan with an outrageous Okie accent. ["When I did what my wife said and opened that cabin door to see a eight-foot grizzly bar a-standin' thar, I had a historical woman on my hands for awhile."]

Also with us were Short Hall, an intense crew-cut Colorado A. & M. forestry student; Hal Samsel, a colorful-talking native of Polson, Montana; and Jack Wall, a second year jumper who spent each academic year working as an able seaman on the seas of the world in the Merchant Marine. Also in our group were Bob Bennett of Paris, Tennessee; Lennie Piper of Blairsville, Pennsylvania; and Henry Thol, Jr., of Kalispell, Montana,---all of whom would die a month later in the Mann Gulch Fire. But at that time life was exhilarating, and we were being flown by the U.S. Forest Service to our unknown work station in the vast Northwest.

In the Doug we flew downstream, that is northwest, above the Clark Fork of the Columbia, into the narrowest part of the Idaho Panhandle (45 miles across), over the beautiful Lake Pend Oreille (pronounced Pond-O-Ray) with its stately islands, past the even more remote and far-flung Priest Lake, and crossed into the northeast corner of Washington State about twenty miles from the Canadian border. There two big mountain ranges below formed a north-south trough, in the bottom of which lay a ten-mile jewel of blue water: Sullivan Lake.

The slopes surrounding the lake were thick with conifers---fir, pine, western larch and spruce---and off the north end of the lake a tiny airstrip had been cleared to support a ranger station. One paved road snaked through the trees ten miles west to the lonesome town of Metaline Falls, the last U. S. town on that road to Canada. That village was on the north-flowing Pend Oreille River---the new name of the Clark Fork after it emerges from Lake Pend Oreille. The water of that river would soon flow into Canada, then take a hard left to the west, re-enter the United States, and add its bit to the main flow of the Columbia River surging south out of the Canadian Rockies.

To prepare Sullivan Lake Ranger Station to let us use their airstrip the pilot first flew over the station revving his engines---mainly to see that they knew we were coming and didn't have any deer on the "runway" or any house-trailers being towed on that road which cuts slantwise across the middle of the strip. Then the pilot swung south over the long cool lake losing altitude, and about halfway down he swung an easy 180 degrees and came back north till he was only fifty feet off the water and flying straight in, flaps down, power on, for a quick grab at the land soon as she came. The strip was thick with grass but flat and level and in relation to the lake-level was almost like that of a carrier deck to the sea.

We met the ranger, were assigned a bunk house, shown where the mess hall was and given the times for dinner and breakfast. ["You make up your own sack lunches from the makin's table after breakfast. But whatever you take you've also got to carry. And no litterin' up of the job site or the roads."] He also warned us about the bears who come frequently to the garbage pit right next to the road from town. And then he told us about the chief attraction of Sullivan Lake Ranger Station in summer: a small county beach with swimming and diving platforms and a few rowboats for rent.

"It's even nice enough that some of the girls come out from town to swim here and frolic in the sun. There's a bus back and forth to town too, but the last one out here from town leaves at 10 PM. If you miss that one, it's a ten mile walk---if you don't lose the road in the dark. Or meet a bear. Or step on a porcupine. Or a skunk. Lots of animals out at night. And they seem to like to use that road. And you're expected to get enough sleep to be able to work hard all day in the hot sun. Got that?"

Yes sir!" <u>Talk about a great place to work</u>.
"And what is that work anyway, sir?"

"Piling brush; that is gathering into piles the
slash from timbersale logging, the limbs lopped off
the fallen trees so the logs can be bucked into
sawmill lengths and put on log-trucks and hauled
to the mill or to town. These piles of brush, in the
cool fall of the year, will be set afire and burned in
order to clear out the logged area for replanting or
natural regeneration."

Yes, I thought. This is the Forest Service---
whose chief business (despite all that talk about
multiple use) is timber sales, to logging companies
and sawmills, to harvest the "crops" of timber
[U.S. Department of Agriculture, remember?] and
provide the wood (and the jobs) for a million
homes in the fast-developing West of the United
States. And we are to go to the logged-over
areas---those great messes left after the slaughter
of a forest---and help clean them up for
regeneration. Several tree types need the sun on
the soil for the tree-seed to germinate. So we
cultivate organized fire in the fall in order to
cultivate seedlings in the spring and fight wild fire
in the summer. And both jobs help keep the forest
green.

So every morning after breakfast we'd grab
our newly sharpened tools, pile into a canvas-
covered stakeside truck (that new covered wagon)
and be hauled out to a recently logged area to
become brush pilots. ["We see the brush; we
pilot."] Two guys usually rode with the foreman-
driver in the cab, and it was there we discovered
that a deer, flushed out by the lumbering truck,

SMOKEJUMPERS, '49
A Photo Essay
by Peter Stackpole

Lightning storm over the mountains. Three strikes hit the ground, while another bolt rambles cloud-to-cloud above. Some of the ground strikes will set fires.

Montana ridges beneath a storm. Below: Suited up
smokejumpers about to jump from a Ford Trimotor. Spotter
lining up the run with handsignals to the pilot.

A young forest fire, out the Ford's noisy window.

Walking on air, on a training jump. From a Ford Trimotor.

Triple delight. Three jumpers coming down.

Suited up jumpers thoughtfully awaiting the big moment.
Man left of center is Jim Tripp of the University
of Washington in Seattle.

Fire on the mountain, as seen from a DC-3 (or C-47).
Below: Foreman-Spotter Bill Wood points out to jumper
Dave Burt where he wants him to land on the next circle
of the jump spot. The plane is the Doug, or DC-3.

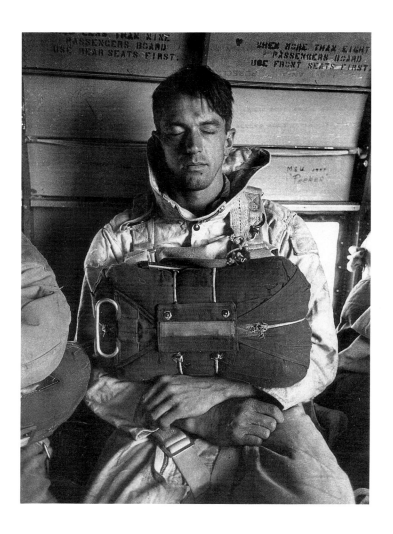

Fred Barnowski, smokejumper foreman, on his way to a fire. Is he dozing? Or praying?

First man out. Static line about to pull off his chute-cover. Second man starting to follow. Plane is the DC-3.

A jumper parts from his mother ship. Note how the apex
of the chute has just parted from the static line
and chute-cover. You're on your own, man.

A smokejumper descends into the smokey forest.

On a fire, a smokejumper hung in a tree starts his rope
let-down. Note harness and reserve left above.

The Ford Trimotor dives to 200 feet to drop firepacks on
a fire.

What it's all about. Fighting fire. Smokejumper on the ground throws a shovel-full of dirt to smother flames.

Cutting fireline and cooling hotspots.

At the end of training Jack Rose of Los Angeles, camp comedian, entertains other jumpers during lunch break on the 70-man "graduation jump" in Hayes Creek Canyon.

Smokejumper trainees do pushups in front of a Ford
Trimotor at Ninemile Airstrip near Huson, Montana.
Man in striped sweater is Hugh Jenkins.

Smokejumper Joe Lee of Spokane swings through the obstacle course---to build arm, hand and upper body strength.

The "Torture Rack"---designed to get the trainees in
shape through exercise of back and stomach muscles.
Closest man on left is Joe Lee of Spokane. Third closest
man on right is Short Hall.

Geronimo! Jumper leaps off the shock tower to learn
what an opening shock feels like. WHAM on
wherever the harness runs.

An experienced smokejumper demonstrates to trainees how to steer a Forest Service parachute. The trainee seated in front of the rope-pullers is Eldon Diettert, who later died in the Mann Gulch Fire.

Three jumper trainees practice rope let-downs from the high cable. The man closest to us has just secured his rope to a belt UNDER his harness, and is tossing his hundred-foot rope toward the ground, preparing to slide down it.

Brothers in the sky. Trainees watch others do high let-downs from a cable above. Center man with cap is Henry Thol, Jr., later killed in Mann Gulch.

Two jumpers coming down over spruce trees. Note the steering slots in the parachute canopies.

Coming in perfect. Jumper about to land in opening among trees.

An eight man squad of jumpers and their spotter, Bob Manchester, pose before the Ford Trimotor that carries them to up to four separate fires in one load. Only the equipment <u>behind</u> Manchester would go on typical smokejumper fires in '49. (The foreground stuff was experimental or specialized equipment, not then in actual use.) The Johnson Flying Service pilot is Slim Phillips, known affectionately as The Madman. The jumpers are, L to R, Will Ruud, Matt Galvin, Monroe DeJarnette, Lloyd Brown, Bill Riskin, Eldon Diettert, Tom Marshall and Starr Jenkins. Note external control cables on plane.

Will Ruud and Bill Riskin demonstrate the basic men and equipment needed for the typical small smoke-jumper fire in 1949---usually a lightning strike way back in the timber. The tail of the Ford Trimotor shows its corrugated aluminum skin. Equipment dropped by cargo chute includes 2 firepacks with tools and rations, a water-can, rolled-up packpump watersack (in case springs are found), a cross-cut saw bowed in a loop, and a large canteen. Note the gloves, rope-pocket and reserve chutes with sheathknife on top.

Riggers in the Parachute Loft carefully inspect reserve
(chest-pack) parachutes that have just come back
from firejumps for re-pack if necessary.

As the Mann Gulch Fire still smokes (August 9, 1949),
Forest Service fire investigators walk over the
rocky slope where thirteen good men died.

Bob Sallee and Walt Rumsey, survivors of the Mann
Gulch Fire, at the Parachute Loft, Hale Field,
Missoula, August 1949.

When wildfire catches a deer, how can men escape?
Mann Gulch aftermath. Dave Navon died near the
large tree right of upper center.

Bob Sallee, youngest smokejumper of '49 and a survivor of the Mann Gulch disaster. He stands in the Parachute Loft at Hale Field, Missoula.

Survivors Walt Rumsey (white shirt) and Foreman
R. Wagner Dodge (under clock) being questioned by
Forest Service officials about the Mann Gulch Fire.

R. Wagner Dodge (left) at Phil McVey's funeral, Ronan, Montana.

Wag Dodge (with handkerchief) at Phil McVey's funeral.
(This photo was in LIFE, August 22, 1949, in a news
spread on the disaster.)

Funeral of Phil McVey at Ronan, Montana. Man in sunglasses at center is Wag Dodge, foreman of the Mann Gulch crew.

Four-point buck burned to death in the Mann Gulch Fire. Twelve smokejumpers plus a fire guard were also killed here.

End of Peter Stackpole's photo essay, SMOKEJUMPERS, '49.

A FEW OTHER PHOTOS
from a SMOKEJUMPER'S ALBUM
'48-'49

Foreman Bill Wood talks 'em down, smokejumper training, Missoula. USFS photo by Ernie Briscoe.

Jack Barrett and Starr Jenkins get checked out by Forest Service spotter Dick Courson before a training jump. The plane is the Noorduyn Norseman flying out of Cave Junction, Oregon. Photo by Paul Block © 1951 <u>The Saturday Evening Post</u>.

Ex-paratrooper Dave Navon gets checked out by Spotter
Chuck Pickard for a training jump. Ninemile Airstrip, near
Huson, Montana, July of '49.   Photo by Starr Jenkins.

Peter Stackpole of LIFE setting up a shot. Will Ruud and
Bill Riskin suited up. Chuck Pickard on gear.
U.S. Forest Service photo by Ernie Briscoe.

Chuck Pickard ready to take up a flight of jumpers and
spot them out the door of the Trimotor Ford. The
tubes under his arm contain small drift chutes to
calculate wind-drift. Ninemile Airstrip, Montana.
Starr Jenkins photo.

Above, nineteen jumpers, about to take off for their trainee graduation jump, early July '49, pose before the DC-3 that will take them there. A month later four of these men were killed in the Mann Gulch Fire: Dave Navon (back row, 4th from right); Marvin Sherman, Henry Thol, Jr., and Newt Thompson (front row, 2nd, 5th, and 6th from left, respectively). The author is back row, end man on right. USFS photo by Ernie Briscoe.

Hugh Jenkins   Starr Jenkins   Kermit Cole just
                                            before we jumped
                                            into Yellowstone

Photos: Left: Oberlin College.
         Center: Bill Shrout, © 1951 Saturday Evening Post.
              Right: Starr Jenkins.

Men who died in the Mann Gulch Fire:

Robert Bennett   Eldon Diettert   James Harrison   William Hellman   Phillip McVey

David Navon   Leonard Piper   Stanley Reba   Marvin Sherman   Joseph Sylvia

Henry Thol   Newton Thompson   Silas Ray Thompson

Photos supplied by the families and loaned from the Earl Cooley collection.

Chuck Pickard   Stan Reba   Joe Sylvia

Skip Stratton   Ed Eggen   Bill Dratz   Bill Hellman
ter their ceremonial jump near the White House in Washington,
'28/49.

notes, top, courtesy Chuck Pickard and Mrs. Andre Anderson.
ottom, USFS print loaned by H.W. "Skip" Stratton.

Brothers in the sky. Going out of a Ford Trimotor.
Photo by Robert Catlin.

could dash ahead of us, even uphill and for quite a
ways, at thirty miles per hour. And a black bear,
so much less graceful looking, could do the same
alongside of us or ahead of us, at <u>forty</u> miles per
hour. And the fastest human can go for a short
dash about 21 miles per hour. Something to think
about when you meet a bear in the forest. Better
to light a match and then a branch and hold it in
front of you. Or stand there cool and clatter a
spoon on a pan. But <u>never</u> run. Unless he's big
and you can climb a small tree faster than he can.

On the job we also discovered that
yellowjackets are not bees exactly but they sting
harder and more often and they live in the ground
in burrows that we tend to uproot as we chop and
fling the brush into piles. So we started calling our
sector Bee Haven, and of course the prettiest
Metaline Falls girl on "our" beach came to be
known---quite undeservedly---as Miss Bee Haven.

We discovered that northeast Washington
has "only about ten days of summer," and "we
just had it"---except that this summer the warm
days hung on so that we actually had about three-
and-a-fourth weeks of fine weather with only a
couple of rains.

After a hard day's work and a good shower
and putting on clean clothes for supper, we
discovered that hummingbirds shop for nectar by
homing in on (homing-birds, get it?) bright colors,
not necessarily the fragrance of flowers. My loud
socks of red, white, blue and yellow became the
first checkpoint for those lovely whirring
scavengers, hunting desperately to get enough
nectar to take them through their comatose nights.

We found that the bus strangely enough
didn't run much on weekends even though those
were the best days we and the town-folk had for
the little beach. So a couple of times we hitch-
hiked to town with hardly any car traffic coming
by to pick us up. If you couldn't get a car or truck
to stop for you and the driver of the lumber-spider
came by, he would likely as not break company
rules and be able to take one hitchhiker only for a
ride.

Now a lumber spider is a bizarre vehicle with
each of its four wheels supporting a tall stilt to
hold the one-seat cab way up off the roadway so
the rig can drive up and straddle a load of finished
lumber, slide big steel flanges under the load, pick
it up, and carry it from the sawmill yard to the
railroad or ten miles to Metaline Falls. But where
can a hitchhiker fit on such a rig?

The driver stops, climbs out of his rear seat,
comes forward, climbs down a ladder on the
outside of his two right stilts, lets you the
hitchhiker climb up and get behind his seat in a
small space and hang on standing; then he climbs
back up the ladder and resumes his driver's seat
and off you go, lumber load or not.

But it only carries one passenger. And only
during daylight hours. But it sure beats walking
ten miles.

Naturally I had to date Miss Bee Haven (thus
proving that she did not deserve that title), and
went in to Metaline Falls on a Saturday night or
two, to take her to the only things going on, a
church dance or social. Of course I missed that
last bus. And of course I walked that dark ten

miles of road. Seeing <u>creatures</u> (raccoons I believe) congregating in the dark, with me hoping
they were not skunks or bear cubs, and generally
sweating profusely as I approached the ranger
station garbage pit part of that road. After a
couple of those treks, I decided less courting and
more sleep were in order.

One weekend four of us, Short Hall, Red
Anderson, Bob Bennett and I, climbed to a nearby
lookout tower, seven miles above the road. It was
the type of lookout with the entire square cabin at
the top of a wooden tower, with balconies all
around and the horizontal shutters raised to form
solar shades for the balconies and the all-around
windows. From this lonesome wooden glass eye a
lookout named George Sand surveyed his awe-
some responsibility and called in any smokes not
previously accounted for.

The dim ridges of Idaho were visible to the
east; the rumpled mountains of Canada to the
north; and one sliver of Sullivan Lake showed
beyond a foreground slope of thick timber. Storm
clouds hung low overhead for awhile but kept on
sliding east with little rain. We listened to George
Sand tell us how the firefinder worked, admired
the staggering views, marveled at the lightning-
storm stool he sits on with the insulator feet, and
we were glad we were not lookouts.

It had taken us almost three hours to hike up
that seven miles. We <u>ran</u> down that lumpy pre-
carious trail in exactly one hour, lucky to have not
broken three legs, four ankles and two arms by
such stupidity. ["Save that for a rescue jump, you
knotheads. We trained you to jump on fires, not

to wreck yourselves running down mountain trails.
You're as bad as those free-fall artists!"
(Smokejumpers who also do free-fall parachute
jumps with their own chutes at county fairs and air
shows on weekends for extra kicks and extra
cash. Of which the Smokejumper Administration
takes a dim view.)]

On the job we became adept at lopping
limbs and flinging branches and building good tree-
limb funeral pyres for the demolished forest, to be
set off just before or after the first snow in
October. In short, hot brush pilots.

Finally July waned and August began and
one day they brought us back to the station right
after lunch. "Okay guys. Pack up your stuff and
clean that bunk house! Missoula just called to say
the Doug is coming out to get you about 4 today."

"Yay." "They didn't forget us!" "Hot
damn!"

"They say you're needed for scrubbin' pots
and pans around that Parachute Loft mess hall
back there. So get this place cleaned up or we'll
keep both you and the plane here another night."

At around 3:55, when the shadow of the
western range was already darkening our grassy
airstrip, over came the beautiful silver DC-3 shining
in the sun. The pilot revved his engines to be sure
we closed that road and ran the deer off the strip,
then he glided down the lake, turned and power-
flew back in, coming in over the water almost
dead-level with the strip. His wheels grabbed the
ground soon as it arrived, and he rolled on in,
actually stopping right on the one paved part of
that whole "airport"---the road which ran slantwise

across the middle of the strip.

   We thanked the ranger and the cook and the other Sullivan Lake strawbosses, loaded up the Doug, and found ourselves seats along the walls forward. The pilot taxied up to the end of the strip, reversed field, watched both sides of that crazy road for traffic and gunned her hell-bent for the lake. The Doug hit the road again, jumped off it into the air, and we were airborne again, climbing above long, blue Sullivan Lake---up into the sun for that great flight, back across many mountain ranges, home to Missoula.

   We were off again, as brothers in the sky. And it was three days before the Mann Gulch Fire.

Smokejumper Diary
(of Hugh Jenkins)

Hughie on Project:

 Last Monday three of us plus our foreman were sent away from that comfortable Sullivan Lake Ranger Station out to a decidedly primitive trail camp some thirteen miles away. This camp, romantically named Gypsy Meadows, consisted of two log cabins in a marsh near a creek, and was inhabited by approximately two dozen porcupines and sixteen million mosquitoes, as well as a worn-out old wino who served as our cook. Oh, the adventurous life of a smokejumper! The mosquitoes were great big persistent monsters, evolved to pester deer; and us humans were pretty easy pickings. They moved in swarms.

 The work itself was good; trail and telephone line maintenance. In the morning we'd crawl out of our sleeping bags, rinse our hands in the icy water of the creek, and put down one of our wino's breakfasts: fried eggs, hot cakes, coffee. After breakfast we'd pick up a saw, a couple of axes, and some climbing spurs and start up one of the many nearby trails. The trails would always be going up, because Gypsy Meadows is in a bottom; and the places trails lead to are lookouts and the lateral ridge trails. Our job was to clear out the tree-trunks fallen across the trail during the winter, and to repair the breaks in the telephone lines to the lookouts. The lookouts aren't manned yet, since the fire season hasn't really started.

The early morning work would be through dark groves of cedar and white pine, very shadowy, dim and damp. The trail would snake between the big pillars of trees, occasionally blocked by a big log lying across, or a snarl of smaller windfalls. We'd saw or chop through, and after a while the sun would strike down through to the decaying duff on the forest floor. Then the trail would start making switchbacks (hairpin turns, we used to call them) as it started up the steep slopes; and the timber would get smaller and lighter green. By this time the mosquitoes would be far behind and below, we would be starting to sweat, and once in a while a break in the trees would give us a view of the more distant ridges as we climbed. By about ten o'clock, ordinarily, we would begin hitting snow, soggy drifts lying across the trail, hard to walk through without sinking in deep.

There would be breaks in the sunny spots, and not much to cut out, so high. Finally we'd reach the lookout, high up in the wind on some ridge. There would always be a great view, the snow-capped Canadian ridges only a few miles

north, maybe a part of Priest Lake to the east, or
the Pend Oreille River to the west, and always the
piled blue rows of mountains behind mountains.

At noon we'd eat our sandwiches and
oranges, carried in the sugar sacks tied to our
belts. A couple of hours from five o'clock we'd
start back down over the trail we'd worked,
walking rapidly past the freshly cut windfalls.
Back in Gypsy Meadows we'd eat supper, try to
wash up a bit while fighting the mosquitoes, and
after an evening of reading or talking, crawl
unshowered and unshaven into our sacks.

Our foreman was Carl. Carl was born in
Minnesota about sixty years ago, German stock,
and has spent a lifetime working in the woods.
He's a short, stocky old wood-tick, with the big
stubby hands of a workman, and he can outwork
any of these twenty-year-old college punks any
day. He's got a profile of a Roman Senator: no
neck, bald, square-headed, with a huge hooked
nose and a solid chin. We've decided he's
invulnerable; you couldn't hit him without
smashing your hand. He's a very kindly and
unassuming old character though, always cracking
that formidable profile into a wheezy little smile. A
good man to work for.

All this is past tense, because this evening
Missoula called for two men. There were three of
us at Gypsy Meadows, so we flipped to see who
would stay. I got to be one of those who will go,
and tomorrow we'll find out what the deal is.

Colville, Washington. July l7th
The deal out here in the Colville has turned

out pretty well, so I'll probably hang on to the job
for the rest of the summer. There are two of us
here, about fifteen miles out of the little town of
Colville; and we're living in a big white nine-room
farmhouse surrounded by pasture and meadow.
The whole valley we're in was once private
farming land, but the FS bought up the whole
works during the thirties, and set aside the best
local farmhouse for its trail camp. So here we are
with plumbing, a big kitchen with woodburning
stove, a green Forest Service pickup to drive
around in, and four goodlooking saddle horses
grazing around the house. The easy-going old
ranger in Colville mentioned that we might give the
horses some exercise; so last Sunday we rode two
of them down to some lakes a few miles from here
and had an afternoon of swimming before bringing
them back. Yep, smokejumping's a tough racket.
The two of us have been working telephone line
and trail around here; so I'm getting a little practice
with climbers, as well as experience in the art of
catching horses, saddling them up, riding them---
besides cooking and driving.

      We're completely out of touch with
Missoula; and what kind of a fire season they are
having I don't know. Presumably not very much
of a one so far. The first fire jump was on the 5th
of July, and on the 8th sixteen men went in the C-
47 clear down to the Boise Forest in Region Four.
They've probably had a few scattered fires since.
I would just as soon stay out here in our
farmhouse for a few more weeks.

Hughie's Glory Days

Note left for Starr:

It's been an active week; and if things keep up like this for the rest of the season, I'll be a rich man---although possibly a gray-headed one. I've gotten sixty-plus hours of overtime in the last seven days, which is about average for everyone in the outfit.

The big bust started in the middle of the week before last. A week ago Friday the two of us at Colville were flown back to Missoula. After hanging around for a day, I was dispatched in a Ford load to the Clearwater Saturday afternoon. The eight of us were to split up to cover four small fires. It was something to be last and watch the other three crews go out. It was late in the afternoon, and a storm was moving in from the southwest while the sun was hitting the peaks north of us and the ranges to the east were shrouded in shadows and scattered blue clouds. The third crew before us jumped on a high ridge

with the storm crawling in on three sides.
Lightning below in the distance, and the
beginnings of rain spattering the windows during
the final pass when the guys stepped out.

We had to dive down through a light mist to
drop the cargo. For our fire, we flew around the
storm and got into a clear area it had just passed
over. We dropped on another high ridge, and I
glanced off the dead top of a big fir and was
flipped head-over-heels for a moment before
straightening out for a soft landing in the brush.

We put out the little fire that night, slept a
little in the cargo chutes (couldn't find the sleeping
bags) and got our stuff together to go out the next
day. The briefing sheet in my map case gave the
instructions for travelling out in seven unfortunate
words: "Down Obia Creek trail to Obia Cabin."
Obia Creek, we figured out from the map, was
about a mile down the slope from the fire; and the
cabin, with grub and telephone, would be about
six miles farther down the trail. Seemed like a
snap. Unfortunately, as the dispatcher in the
Lochsa Ranger Station nervously told us later, he
was new on the district, and didn't know that Obia
Creek trail had been abandoned for ten years.
As it was, we spent five hours Monday morning
moving all our gear down the slope to the so-called
trail. The slope, passably steep, was so completely covered and clogged with brush and
reproduction that we had to make two trips---
sliding and stumbling at every step, our boots
sliding off the green limbs, the packs constantly
throwing us off balance, our lower legs getting
mauled and scratched by the antagonistic green

stuff we'd been called to jump in there to protect.
We sweated gallons. The trail had been well
treaded by game where we hit it; so after lunch (a
can of soup apiece), we started hopefully down it
with our jump suits on our backs.

It didn't take long to find out that the trail,
except for a few antique blazes, was non-existent.
So there we were---crawling over huge seven-foot
cedar windfalls, falling into mudholes, wading the
rock-bottomed creek over our boot-tops again and
again. This kept up for about four miles. About
an hour before dark we got out of it to where the
trail was maintained and tramped wearily down the
remaining two miles to the cabin. I called the
ranger from the cabin, and he made a half-hearted
apology for the mixup and told us to walk on in to
the ranger station in the morning. That was
another six miles for us Tuesday, still packing our
suits; but of course that walk was relatively
pleasant. We flew back to Missoula from Orofino,
Idaho, on Tuesday afternoon.

Everything at Missoula was a continuous
mass of confusion. On Wednesday morning I was
fortieth on the jump list, but by Wednesday
afternoon I was off again in the Ford, this time part
of an eight-man crew heading for the Bitterroot.
Half the guys in the plane were reading their mail
and making out overtime slips from the last fire.

We jumped in a stand of tall timber about
two miles above the Salmon River. I've concluded
that mature yellow pine is dangerous stuff to jump
into. Two of our crew were hurt, both of them by
having their canopies spilled by the limbs without
hanging up. One boy, named Forbes, plowed

down through the branches for eighty feet and
cracked both his ankles as well as wrenching his
knee and bruising his back. Another, the
squadleader, Wilkerson, did the same thing and
fouled up his shoulder somehow. My own
experience made me damned nervous. I smashed
down into one of the big pines, and ended up in
the limbs, head down, with my legs hooked over
one branch and another under my back. The
shock came when I looked up and saw that the
chute was barely hung up, merely by a few dead
tips, and that all my weight was supported by the
network of limbs I'd landed in. I clumsily worked
my way up astride one of the branches and made
my letdown with the rope cinched around the tree,
using sixty-five feet of my rope in the process.

By this time it was approaching dark, and it
was too late to take the hurt men out that night.
We made a stretcher out of a sleeping bag and got
the casualties together to do what we could for
them. Wilkerson was vomiting and had a cut on
his forehead, and at first it was kind of painful for
him to lie prone; but eventually he went to sleep.
He's in the hospital now, and apparently it's
nothing permanently serious. Forbes's ankles were
obviously dislocated and he had pains in his knee
and back, and in general he spent a miserable
night. He, too, is all right now---the back and knee
pains were just bruises. One ankle was broken,
and the other badly sprained. We worked all night
to clear a spot for the helicopter, knocking over ten
or twelve big yellow pines (pitchy as hell, and
working without wedges), and we cleared an
avenue of approach and takeoff so that the copter

could come in and perch on a level spot on the ridge.

The copter, together with another Ford load, came in soon after daylight. The Ford crew jumped while the copter buzzed around. Cochran spotted the men one at a time from five hundred feet, and got everyone in without hanging up. While the men were coming down, Forbes was pretty agitated. He kept muttering that somebody was going to land on him. He and Wilkerson were lying side by side in the middle of the spot.

Then the copter buzzed in, and it was really a sight to see that huge bug come in and settle on that dinky little spot high above the Salmon, with the great fallen trees lying on the slopes just below it.

The copter buzzed away with the patients, one at a time; and we settled down to the routine of mopping up the fire (which had luckily died down during the night) and waiting for the ground pounders to arrive. Yesterday, Saturday, we walked out. It was a good twenty miles, but a fine trail all the way; no need to carry anything but lunches, and a cool overcast made it an easy trip. We rode an old rattly schoolbus back to Missoula, and got here at I AM this morning.

Well, I hope this recitation of my adventures doesn't seem long-winded. Remember, you asked for it. I could go on for some time, because the past week has produced a tremendous crop of stories. But I've got to stop. Be seeing you in a few days.

Your bro,

Hugh

Trapped in the Firestorm

This chapter is based mostly on Earl
Cooley's <u>Trimotor and Trail</u> (1984), p. 83-131,
plus my own recollections of what survivors Walt
Rumsey and Bob Sallee said around camp after this
disaster. Earl Cooley was one of the first two
smokejumpers to jump on a forest fire in July
1940, and he went on to become the leader of the
Missoula smokejumpers for 13 years, including
1949. He also was the chief spotter on the Mann
Gulch Fire and as such took responsibility for
putting the 15 jumpers down where he did in what
became, two hours later, the valley of death.
Another source has been Norman Maclean's
exhaustive study of the Mann Gulch Fire, <u>Young
Men and Fire</u> (1992). Another has been Richard C.
Rothermel's scientific paper, "Mann Gulch Fire: A
Race that Couldn't be Won," USDA-FS Gen-Tech
Report INT-299, May 1993. The following chapter
also relies on these sources.

                    *   *   *

The disastrous story of the Mann Gulch Fire
can be told in a few pages. Mann Gulch is the
rough, rocky ravine that taught the smokejumpers
with a vengeance what they already intuitively
knew: That wildfire in the explosive stage is a lot
more dangerous than mere treetop mountain flying,
or air-cargo dropping, or tree climbing with belt
and spurs, or using sharp-edged tools in long lines
of swinging men cutting through a forest---or even
than parachute-jumping itself. This fire also re-
taught the smokejumpers that when a fire decides
to blow up in your face, it can kill you and your
whole crew in less than two minutes. It also
taught them several new-old concepts like flash
fuels (this one appropriately named cheat-grass),
fighting fire with fire (here called an escape fire),
sudden death through complete oxygen-loss
combined with sudden heat (up to and over 1000
degrees), whirlwinds of fire (the only precise
meaning of the commonly misused word firestorm), and the possibility of quickly-killed men
being strewn across a flame-ravaged mountain-
slope for almost a quarter of a mile.

Mann Gulch---even the name seems appro-
priate---is a usually dry two-and-a-half mile
drainage feeding into the Missouri River just before
she emerges from the Northern Rocky Mountains
at a place Lewis and Clark called the Gates of the
Mountains. The Gates was the deep river-cleft in
the first big range of the Rockies that Lewis and
Clark encountered on their epic up-river voyage.
At this point the Missouri is flowing roughly north
out of southwestern Montana where the river has

been gathering its mighty waters from a thousand mountain streams and snow-fields. Most of this flow converges about 25 miles north of Helena, the capital of Montana, where a minor empty gulch snakes in from the east to join the sizeable Missouri in its majestic surge toward the faraway sea.

As in much of the interior West, the north-facing slopes of this gulch are thickly timbered, the south-facing ones covered with scattered lodge-pole pines and range grasses---here fescue and cheat-grass, one of the fastest burning grasses known.

Since the area has very few roads and no settlements, much of it has been designated by the Forest Service as Gates of the Mountain Wilderness. And even on the parts between the Wilderness and the river, the Forest Service has been keeping the cows out to return it to its natural state. This in turn has caused the formerly sparse grass to come back in knee high and slippery when you try to run through it. The land belongs to the government; the jurisdiction is the Helena National Forest; and all these factors make Mann Gulch smokejumper country even though it is just a couple of drainages from the start of the Great Plains.

August 3, 1949: On the faraway sun, a huge sunspot erupts, sending out 250,000-mile flames to lash at the white hot pitch-black space. From the sunspot cauldron pour gusher-storms of radiation to flash extra energy outward through space to the faraway planets. Including the blue and white one 93 million miles out.

*   *   *

Wednesday, August 3, 1949, at the dirt airstrip just outside the village of West Yellowstone, Montana; lodgepole pine country, 6 PM.

It's still bright sunlight and a warm afternoon, and the old Ford Trimotor is coming in for a landing. Bill Hellman and Bob Bennett, both tall men, have been stomping around the refueling area for an hour to release their pent-up frustration at missing a jump today---and having to wait, wait, wait. It is Bill Hellman's 24th birthday but this is a fairly rotten birthday present. The plane settles on its big truck tires and soon trundles over to gas up.

Bill Hellman, handsome, married and just five weeks a father, is one of the best of Missoula's squadleaders. He and three others of his experienced type were flown from Missoula back to Washington, D.C. a few weeks ago for a Forest Service media event. (It took them three days each way in the slow-flying Ford---especially since the Trimotor does not fly at night.) They went to parachute-jump as smokejumpers on the Ellipse between the Washington Monument and the White House---hoping that President Harry Truman would come out of the kitchen to see them----as Forest Service emissaries to industrial leaders, to thank them for their support of forest fire prevention programs. Of course the industrial leaders really should have been thanking the smokejumpers for doing the hot, hard work out on the ground. But this kind of harmless flummery is something the Forest Service can do, but can never call public relations. It goes under the bureaucratic rubric of I. and E.---Information and Education.

And Bill Hellman was jumping near the White House in Washington the day after his wife Gerry gave birth to their son in Kalispell, Montana.

Back here in West Yellowstone, Spotter Hank Shank is the first one off the plane, ready to help the pilot with the refueling. Next emerges the Park Ranger, slightly airsick and glad to be on solid ground again. He is followed by Lenny Piper and Henry Thol, both also irked by having missed a jump but needing to stretch their legs and shed their chutes and jump-suits after the long flight.

The ranger says to Shank, "Sorry, Hank, that we couldn't find that third fire. We were sure it was there this morning."

"Maybe a geezer put it out," says Hank. "Don't worry. It happens every day."

"And Bill," says the Park man to Hellman. "Thanks a lot for the use of your harness and chute. I'd have probably fallen out without them."

"You're quite welcome," says Hellman, unsnapping the harness and adjusting it back to his size. "But I sure missed leaping on that other blaze today myself. And Bennett too."

"Yeah," says Bob Bennett from Paris, Tennessee. "A long way to come for a dry run."

"Well we sure appreciate you guys in the FS bein' ready to help when our lightning fires start a-poppin'," says the ranger.

"Don't mention it," says Shank. "All in the game."

The ranger shakes hands with Shank and the rest of the crew and waves his thanks to the busy pilot. The pilot has just emerged and is hustling to get those gas-hoses into his tanks.

"Hank!" he says. "Run over to the Airport
Cafe and pick up the sandwiches and coffee I
radioed in for. We've gotta get back to Missoula
before dark. You know these Fords don't like to
land at night."

"I've already got 'em," says Hellman. "You
guys get over there to the out-house and get right
back here to load up. Let's go!"

A few minutes later all are back and the
plane re-loaded, and the pilot starts his still-warm
engines, taxies to the end of the strip, turns, and
takes off.

Thus do the first four smokejumpers, Bill
Hellman, Bob Bennett, Len Piper and Henry Thol,
Jr., begin their two-stage journey to Mann Gulch.

Thursday, August 4. Lots of fires going
around Region One's 16 national forests, with
plenty of cargo-dropping and several flights out of
Missoula to bring in smokejumpers from their
various outlying work projects. But no new
firejump calls come in. The four jumpers rejoin the
others who are still putting the new green tarpaper
roof on the Parachute Loft at Hale Field while they
wait impatiently for the next fire call to come. It's
a good thing they're working hard because most of
the planes are still out and they couldn't all go
today anyway.

Friday, August 5, 1949. Another blazing
hot day in Missoula and in Helena too. At 1:50
PM from the Helena National Forest the call comes
in. Jack Nash, fire dispatcher at the Parachute
Loft, takes the call and hears that Bob Jansson,

ranger of the Canyon Ferry District on the Helena,
has a fire going in Mann Gulch near the Gates of
the Mountain. Jack is soon locating it on one of
his big maps.

"We think it is a 50-man fire already, so we
need at least 25 smokejumpers right away. We'll
get a ground crew on it as soon as we can."

With all the other big planes out, only one
plane is available: a Douglas DC-3, aerial work-
horse of the world in the 30's and 40's. A good
plane, but it carries only 16 jumpers with all their
fire-gear and needed spotters. "Well 16 is a good
start. Send them right away, and whatever others
you can send later."

Fifteen jumpers are called off their roofing
job. "Hellman, Bennett, Piper, Thol! Diettert,
Navon, McVey, Sherman! Thompson-Newton;
Thompson-Ray! Joe Sylvia, Merle Stratton (that's
Merle Stratton not Skip Stratton), Walt Rumsey,
Bob Sallee, and Stan Reba of Brooklyn, New
York!"

R. Wagner Dodge, universally known among
the jumpers as Wag, one of the best of the jump
foremen, is to lead this crew. That makes sixteen.
And Bill Hellman, one of the best of the squadleaders, is to be their squadleader or assistant
foreman.

Fred Stillings, R-1's air operations officer, a
little perturbed that this fire is so suddenly much
bigger than most smokejumper fires, calls Earl
Cooley, head of the smokejumper project.

"Earl, will you spot this one? And let me
know how many more men you need. We don't
want this one wiping out that campground in

Meriwether Canyon [where Meriwether Lewis made his first camp in the Rocky Mountains]---or the Gates of the Mountain Wilderness."

So that puts three of the most experienced men in leading positions on what still looks to be a routine fire---except that it is already 30 or 40 acres big---far larger than the usual two-man smokejumper lightning-strike fire.

About noon over in Meriwether Camp-ground, next canyon up the Missouri from Mann Gulch, Fire Guard James O. Harrison, 20 years old of Missoula, is the lone man in charge. It's not a heavily used campground since it is only reachable by boat on the river. Jim is worried about the smoke billowing along the ridge to the north. Also the radio to headquarters is not working due to heavy sunspot static these last couple of days. But Jim doesn't need orders from Ranger Bob Jansson, who has been flying over assessing this new lightning-fire, to know he should get up there with shovel and pulaski and do what he can to keep it from coming over the ridge and down into Meriwether Canyon.

Jim Harrison is a hard worker and a good firefighter and he scrambles up the steep trail 1500 feet to the ridge with tools in hand. Just last year, 1948, he was a successful Missoula smokejumper himself; successful except that it was a wet fire season with very few firejumps for anybody. But Jim Harrison's mother worried that smokejumping was too dangerous a summer job for him, so in deference to her he didn't re-apply this year but got a safer job as a campground fire guard and maintenance man at Meriwether Camp-

ground out here along the Missouri River north of
Helena.

And now he is up along the ridge between
Meriwether Canyon and Mann Gulch, digging fire
trail all by himself, to keep the fire moving gently
northeast and thus not coming over into his
canyon. He has been doing this for two-and-a-half
hours when the smokejumper plane comes in
under squadrons of puffy cumulus clouds from the
west.

"Hey, it's a Doug! It must be the jumpers!
Hi guys! Boy, am I glad to see you!" He moves
out ahead of the slowly-spreading fire, waving his
shovel to his brothers in the sky. Even away from
the fire the temperature is 102 degrees.

Up in that plane, which has been bouncing
roughly over the hot-day up-drafts over the
Continental Divide, Earl Cooley and Wag Dodge are
stretched out full length on the floor, peering out
the open door with goggled eyes, assessing the
fire and the spotting situation. Earl always uses
this safety-first flat-on-the-floor stance since on his
very first firejump nine years before---the first
firejump ever made by anyone anywhere---the
spotter fell halfway out the door of the plane
without a chute and very nearly didn't make it
back in. Wag in deference to Earl uses the same
technique today, though no other spotters are
quite this cautious about standing near the door.

The jumpers are all suited up, checked out,
with static lines in their hands, helmets on with
facemasks buckled down. But the bumpy air and
constant buffeting has several of them airsick and

woozy. The twelfth man on the crew, Merle
Stratton, a third year jumper, is sicker than most---
something that has been happening to him on
every jump lately---something that he has had
about all he can take of. Suddenly a wave of
nausea sweeps over him and he throws up into his
facemask.

He rips off his mask and starts wiping it out
with his gloves and says something like, "Earl!
Wag! I'm not gonna jump today! Or ever! I've
had it with this goddam bumpy airsickness!"

"Is it that bad, Merle?"

"It's that bad. I"m goin' back to Missoula
and quit! Today! Sorry Chief, but it ain't fun any
more."

"Okay, Merle. Here's some clean rags.
We're sorry to lose you, man. Especially now."

So right there in the plane, above the gently
burning fire in Mann Gulch, the 16-man crew
shrinks to 15. But then a few minutes later, after
all of those 15 make it safely to the ground
through the hot thermal-battered air, Wag Dodge
finds the hard-working Jim Harrison coming around
the head of the fire from the ridge to meet them.
And Harrison, a jumper from the previous year,
knows many of them, and they know him; and the
crew is sixteen smokejumpers again.

So Merle Stratton escapes Mann Gulch at
the last moment through no fault of his own. And
Jim Harrison, already in Mann Gulch as a firefighter, rejoins his brothers in the sky.

And for the rest of her life, Jim Harrison's
mother will mourn.

*   *   *

As Earl and Wag survey the fire from the plane it is 50 to 60 acres, moving slowly northeast along the Mann Gulch side of the ridge. It looks non-threatening and quite normal, and since the ridge dips into a saddle just ahead of the fire, they expect it will slow down as it burns down-slope into the saddle---especially since the late afternoon often begins to cool a fire about this time and slow it down.

So they pick the safest jump spot---a grassy slope across the gulch-bottom and upgulch, about 3/4 of a mile from the head of the fire. From their drift chutes they estimate the ground winds to be less than 15 miles per hour and thus quite safe for jumping. Then Wag Dodge and Bill Hellman lead the men out in the first of four sticks about 3:10 PM. The last men jump a few minutes later and all land safely except Wag Dodge who has a hard landing, putting a puncture wound down to the bone in one elbow.

Because of the very rough air, the pilot requires that they drop the cargo from the normal jump altitude (1000 feet) rather than the usual cargo dives to 200. Thus the cargo is widely scattered and takes a long time to gather up. And one cargo chute fails to open. The crucial item smashed on landing is their two-way radio.

While they are gathering chutes, tools and supplies into a cache near the gulch-bottom, Wag Dodge tells Hellman to have the crew finish the gathering, eat a quick supper out of their food supply, and move on south across the gulch and up to where he, Wag, is going to talk to the fire guard [Harrison] who is coming down the slope

from in front of the fire to join them. Since this
man will know about any ground crew on the other
side of the fire, he is the first man Dodge needs to
talk to.

As he crosses the gulch bottom and climbs
to meet Harrison, Dodge worries about the thickets
of small trees he is passing through---ripe fuel for a
flash blow-up if the wind changes. He meets and
talks to Harrison---an acquaintance from last year--
-finds out there is no other ground crew yet, and
decides that this angle of attack on the fire is all
wrong since there is so much thick reproduction
(small timber) close to the ground on this side.

He shouts down to Hellman, who is now
about 100 yards this side of the gulch-bottom with
the men all tooled up, to have him reverse course
and take all hands back across gulch and angle
west (left) toward the river to start their fire-line
there. Meanwhile he and Harrison will go down to
the supply cache, grab a quick supper and catch
up with them shortly.

If this preoccupation with eating seems
strange to the reader, remember that these men
are right at their normal supper time at the end of
a full day's work already, and that they expect to
be doing hard labor for the next sixteen hours as
they chop fire-line around a sixty-acre fire all night
and into the morning. They themselves will need
all the fuel they can get for the next twelve hours
till breakfast. Little do they know that most of
them will die in the next hour. And for those who
don't it will be a very fierce night.

Hellman takes the men back across the

gulch-bottom and left (west) toward the river,
angling up the slope as they go to get into thinner
timber and more grass. Dodge and Harrison soon
catch up with them and Dodge resumes the lead
with Hellman dropping to the rear. While they are
moving west the fire still seems to most of the
men to be not dangerous, though the wind coming
into their faces from the river now has clearly
picked up.

Suddenly Dodge notices a strange thing.
Downgulch ahead of them in the bottom new
smoke is roiling up from what must be spotfires,
started by flying embers thrown into the winds
eddying off of the main fire above. But the wind
pushing the main fire seems wrong for that
direction of eddy. But there is that new smoke.
And it's really boiling. So suddenly their march to
the river for safety in line-building is cut off. The
way the wind from the river is flowing, those spot
fires will soon merge and spread this way fast. So
Dodge, surveying the scene, at 5:45 reverses the
direction of march again---but still keeps angling up
the slope on the north side of the gulch, to try to
get out of this new fire's likely path. This is his
second change of direction in thirty minutes, and
the men are starting to get nervous.

Now the slope of Mann Gulch on this side is
about 33 degrees---so steep as to make one pause
before trying to run up it when it's hard enough to
walk up it at an angle, with the surface lumpy with
rocks and the cheat grass slick. So Dodge keeps
them walking fast away from the new fire in hopes
that they can evade its rapidly building cauldron of
flame. Strangely, as the fire emerges out of the

timber into the cheat grass, it starts moving toward them much faster. The wall of flame is solid and higher than a man's head.

By eight minutes later (5:53) it is obvious that the fire is going to overtake them, and soon. Dodge orders them to drop tools, watercans, foodpacks, cross-cuts and urges them to continue the march in the same direction: northeast angling up out of the gulch.

By now there is so much smoke, "flapping winds," and fire-roar that everything is confused. But it is highly likely that immediately after dropping tools individual men realize they must start running now, cutting around the line of march, to have any hope of making the ridge and possible escape. And as several disappear in the swirling smoke, Dodge, believing all are still in line behind him, orders the men near him to wait and follow him into a burned-out area he will soon make. He then quickly sets fire to the grass ahead of him to get an "escape fire" going.

The north slope fire is now less than 100 yards behind them and the wind is gusting upgulch at 30 to 40 miles per hour. When Wag sets his fluttering book-match in the dry grass, in thirty seconds half an acre of cheat grass explodes away in flame. He immediately starts yelling and waving his arms to get his men to follow him into this still burning burned-out area.

Walt Rumsey, Bob Sallee, Bill Hellman and Eldon Diettert, the men closest to Wag Dodge, see what Wag is doing, but Rumsey thinks whatever it is it's crazy. Between gusts of smoke, Rumsey has been eyeing a place for him to sprint for, and his good buddy Bob Sallee and Eldon Diettert think the same.

Somebody shouts, "To hell with that! I'm getting out of here!" And everybody not already gone bolts upgulch, trying to outrun an eight-foot wall of flame that is coming at them faster then a deer can run.

Rumsey goes for the ridge, keeping his eye on the place where he last saw it through the billowing smoke, racing up the right side of Dodge's escape fire---which because of the peculiar vagaries of wind near big fires is racing up the hill at a 45 degree angle to the left of the track of the main north-slope fire.

Bob Sallee, youngest jumper in camp at 17, is racing behind Rumsey on his left, and Eldon Diettert is doing the same on his right. With all the superhuman strength of all-out adrenalin-drive they make it to a 12-foot-high wall of rim-rock that runs along the slope just below the top of the ridge itself. This wall is too tall and too steep to climb, but Rumsey spots a crevice in it, and Sallee scrambles through with Rumsey right behind him. Eldon Diettert, however, a tall forestry student with a good mind, looks at the crevice and decides it is nothing but a trap, and he races to the right along the face of the rim-rock, looking for a larger opening. In the one minute remaining to him he does not find it.

Meanwhile, back at his escape fire, Wag Dodge, unable to get any of his men to follow him, sees the last few flee on by him, and he moves into the middle of his burned-out area, lies down on the still-sputtering ashes, wets his handkerchief

from his canteen and breathes through it, hugging
the ground in his search for oxygen and cooler air.
As the raging wall of flame comes to his pod of
burn, it divides and flutters looking for more ready-
burnables and does not find them right in the pod.
But the winds and suction of that oxygen-
devouring monster all around the pod are enough
to pick Dodge up off the ground and flop him back
down on it two or three times as successive
waves of fire battle for his soul.

Far up the slope, Rumsey and Sallee
scramble through their crevice in the rim-rock,
make it to the ridge wondering why Diettert did
not follow, race up the ridge to the right a hundred
yards or so, and plunge down the other side
looking for any place that will not burn. There
they find the only other place on these doomed
slopes that fits that description, a rockslide
"several hundred feet long and perhaps seventy-
five feet wide." There they cringe and pant and
move from end to end and side to side of the rock
slope as the fire waves swirl down first on one
side, then the other, then as a raging pincers
moving down both sides together. But the
rockslide is enough, and they do not perish from
heat, flame, oxygen-loss, poison gases, or burning
clothes.

Ranger Robert Jansson, who is coming up
from the river-end of Mann Gulch at this same time
to meet the jumpers and scout the fire, is driven
back and very nearly killed by the same blow-up.
He retreats back to the river, gets out in his boat,

backs out into the river, and sees [as he later writes:] "a wall of flame 600 feet high . . . roll over the ridge and down the other side and continue over ridges and down gulches until [it] . . . covered 3000 acres in ten minutes or less. Anything caught in the direct path of the heat blast perished."

So Mann Gulch becomes a freakish, monster fire---far fiercer than 99% of all other wildfires. And sixteen smokejumpers just happen to be caught in the middle of it.

This huge fire, racing through flash fuels on a hot wind-driven evening, generates (in the opinions of several fire experts) the phenomena known as fire whirls. Fire whirls are small tornadoes of superheated but as-yet-unburned gases, forced from the fuels by the waves of heat flying up the slopes ahead of the fire, yet not ignited since the gas eruptions have gotten ahead of the flames or the oxygen supply. When all three necessaries (fuel-gases, heat and oxygen) finally coincide, the fire blow-up occurs, even though unattached to any fire or fuel below---and a veritable whirlwind of fire rages through the sky wherever the wind and its own internal physics take it.
These fire whirls are now raging all around the helpless crew trapped in Mann Gulch, so that even the havens they are racing to find are already leaping into flame. The malevolent arms of the fire-monster are wrapping around them from all sides and only three are now known to be alive.

*   *   *

On the faraway sun, the sun-spot flame-storm has collapsed back into its writhing pit, and the fountain of radiation which has been bathing Earth and fouling up radio transmissions over the Continental Divide in western Montana now ebbs away.

The Naming of Rescue Gulch

By 6:05 that holocaust afternoon of August 5, 1949, thirteen good men are lost in the smoke and flame. We only know at this point that three have escaped---the foreman by intelligent defensive action, the other two by great determination, intense concentration, incredible running and several marvelous gifts of sheer luck. Luck that they were near the head of the line and thus highest on the hill to start with. Luck that they found a crevice in the rimrock when others could not. Luck that they were together as buddies and helped each other pick the goal and keep going when either one alone might have been unsure or faltering. Luck that they reached the ridge and got on the other side ahead of the flames---into what from this night forward will always be called Rescue Gulch. And the greatest luck of all, that they there found the only rockslide on the mountain big enough to save them.

At 6:10 R. Wagner Dodge feels that the inferno has passed far enough by for him to safely stand up. He does so, brushes himself off, and is glad to see that nowhere is he burned nor are his clothes even scorched. He hears a shout to the east and moves off through the sputtering ashes a couple of hundred feet to find Joe Sylvia. Joe is badly burned on his hands, arms and face, and yet he seems to not be in great pain. The burns are too deep and his shock too great. (Maclean describes him as being euphoric.) Dodge moves him to the shelter of a large rock and makes him as comfortable as possible by clearing an area of rocks, removing his boots from his swelling feet and retrieving his canteen and giving him a drink. Then Dodge tells Joe that he is going to get him some help as soon as possible. Without a radio that may be quite a while.

For the next seven-and-a-half hours Joe Sylvia will be alone in the glittering night, mortally wounded by flames, with a half-full canteen that he cannot lift to his blackened lips.

*   *   *

When the fire burning down from the north ridge of Mann Gulch roars and reaches for them but fails to destroy them, Walt Rumsey and Bob Sallee know they now will make it. When the fire burns out around them and the smoke clears about 6:30, they yell to see if anyone else has made it too.

As they look upslope (east) an answering shout comes from their right or south. They move 30 yards in that direction and find Bill Hellman sitting on a large rock. He is badly burned on his

face, arms, legs and back, and he is in terrible
pain. His shirt is gone as is the back side of his
pants. He tells them he was caught by the flames
right at the ridge and staggered down this far to
try to make for the river. He asks them to do
away with him because he knows he will die. All
they have to give him is water from a canteen but
they try to give him hope as well. They stretch
him out on a big flat rock to keep him out of the
ashes, and Sallee climbs back to the ridge hoping
to retrieve the crew's dropped first aid kit. But the
other slope down into Mann Gulch is still too hot
to go into. As Sallee comes back down, they hear
another shout from above. It is Dodge, bringing
them the wonder of his unburned self and the
news of the fire-ravaged Joe Sylvia. And no news
of the rest of the crew.

Though they don't speculate, all are hoping
that the other eleven are safe in some rockslide
like theirs. Yet the condition of Hellman and Sylvia
gives them all an awful fear.

Dodge decides that he and Sallee should set
out for the river to get help, leaving Rumsey there
to care for Hellman as best he can---and basically
to keep him from trying to crawl for the river to
get more water. The Missouri is visible coursing
along about a mile below them, and Rumsey's half-
empty canteen won't last long in the face of
Hellman's burning thirst.

As they hike through sputtering coals to the
edge of the fire and then on down to the river,
Dodge and Sallee realize anew how great a loss
they suffered when that cargo-chute failed and the
radio smashed. And then of course when this

mission started, they had expected to join up with
a ground crew that was supposedly also rushing
from Helena to the scene. So the Loft did not
provide them with the usual maps and compasses.

And now when they arrive at the river, they
are not sure which way they should hike to get to
the nearest phone or radio. They decide to go
downstream (north) because they had caught a
glimpse of a ranch 3 or 4 miles up Elkhorn Creek in
that direction. And they plant a shovel vertically
into the riverbank with a red bandanna on it, as a
signal for any possible search party or fire-crew
coming down or up the river by boat.

Meanwhile District Ranger Robert Jansson,
after many difficulties and frustrations in rounding
up pick-up firefighters, equipment, supplies, boats
and foremen, has finally gotten a totally
inexperienced crew of not fifty but nineteen men,
assembled hastily from the bars of Helena, at the
Meriwether Guard Station. He has sent them up
the steep trail to the ridge under Alternate Ranger
Hersey. Their orders are to build and hold enough
fireline to keep the fire from coming any farther
down into Meriwether Canyon (an ominous fat
tongue of the fire has already licked over the ridge
for a number of acres), and to link up with Harrison
and the jumpers so they can all get back in
coordinated fashion.

Ranger Jansson, his guard cabin crowded
with river-boaters and would-be volunteer fire-crew
members, has just called Missoula by radio to get
the jumpers' location. The radio is still suffering
from static and interference but he finds that yes

the jumpers did land about 3:30 but no they
haven't radioed out any present location or other
info. Jansson is hoping they have pulled back to
some camp on Willow or Elkhorn Creek after that
terrible blow-up and he is hoping to hear their radio
traffic any time. And then, as night descends at
8:50, into the guard cabin walk Wag Dodge and
Bob Sallee.

From then on the rescue becomes job no. 1
and the fire becomes job no. 2. Jansson leaves
Hersey and another assistant ranger with the fire's
south (or ridge) side, hopes that others will get
good overhead and crew on the fire's east and
north sides---leaving the river to hold it on the
west---while he takes over that rescue. After
several more fiascos of assembling litters, litter
bearers, two doctors and their supplies, not
enough blankets, boats pulling into the wrong
gulch, and too many tourists volunteering to be
rescuers, Jansson launches his small fleet from
Meriwether and other boat landings. Dodge
eventually guides the four boats to the mouth of
the newly named Rescue Gulch about 11 PM.
Jansson calls the roll to pick his 12 man rescue
party from the crowd now ashore, sends the rest
back upriver, and at 11:30 starts up the hill.
The sturdy Bob Sallee is their guide as they
trudge through the night up to where Hellman cries
for water and Sylvia teeters on a rock already
almost beyond pain. Wag returns by boat to
Meriwether to try to organize larger efforts to find
all his missing men.

      *   *   *

About midnight back up at Hellman's big-flat-rock stretcher, Rumsey and he are long out of water. So to quiet Hellman's incessant pleas, Rumsey agrees to hike down to the river to refill the canteen, and he'll be back just as quick as he can. He starts down through the spark-laden night and about a third of the way down sees the lights of the rescue party coming up. He gives a shout. They reply and come on up to his waning light; and Rumsey, Sallee and Jansson push on ahead of the rest to reach the stricken Hellman about 12:35 AM. About six-and-a-half hours of hanging here burned.

Bill's condition is bad. He complains of cold and is very thirsty. They let him rinse out his mouth and drink a little water. When the doctors arrive ten minutes later, they give him a shot of pain-killer, a quart of blood plasma, salve on his burns, and put him on a litter wrapped in the one blanket.

Ranger Jansson figures they had better not try to carry Hellman down over this rocky country in the dark---and possibly get somebody else injured or burned on the way---so he picks out his two best men, Sallee and Don Roos, assistant ranger from the Lincoln District, for the next effort: To climb up over the ridge in this flickering, tree-exploding night and find the equally suffering Joe Sylvia. They top the ridge about 1:20 AM, find their way down over the 12-foot rimrock, and prowl through the sparking burn for 30 minutes till they hear a cry not far below. It takes them ten more minutes to locate Joe Sylvia of Plymouth, Mass, ex-marine, now exuding horrific odors of burned flesh. They find him standing teetering on a large rock, hardly able to keep his balance. They get him to sit down and give him some water, and Jansson peels an orange and feeds it to him one section at a time.

It is 2:20 AM when the doctors arrive and start treating him.

As it starts to get light a little after 4 AM, Jansson gets the six who are slated to take turns carrying out Joe Sylvia to spread out as they move down Mann Gulch to see if they will find anyone else on the way. At 4:30 Jansson himself encounters the first body.

From the glasses, the Catholic emblem, the Forest Service key #18 and the remains of the snakebite kit he himself had given him, Ranger Robert Jansson can tell for sure that these remains are those of his hard-working fire guard, the ex-smokejumper from Missoula, young James O. Harrison. Harrison, who will be forever twenty, has forever rejoined his brothers in the sky.

Joe Sylvia and Bill Hellman are finally carried into the hospital in Helena about 10 AM and 10:30 respectively. But before noon, of kidney failure and severe burns, both die. The doctor who treated them out on the mountain estimates that because of the severity of their burns both young men would have "most certainly" died even if they had been gotten to a hospital and under a doctor's care immediately.

After the carry-out, Ranger Jansson goes

back to Meriwether where he finds a good fire
boss for those east and north flanks of the fire.
Wag Dodge by 7 AM has called Missoula Fire
Control and orders up Region One's sole
helicopter, including pilot Jack Hughes and his
crew of jumpers, all of whom have been stationed
in Moose Creek, Idaho, in the Bitterroot
Wilderness, researching the effectiveness of a
helicopter for back-country fire control. Missoula
Fire Control immediately grants Wag's request, but
it takes a long time to call Moose Creek, alert the
crew, fly the craft back to Missoula (with the crew
in a separate airplane), refuel and resupply it, and
send it out to the mouth of Elkhorn Creek where
some of a larger body-search crew can come in by
road.

     Jansson and Dodge, bringing ten gallons of
water and 24 lunches to support the body-
gathering crew, reach the mouth of Elkhorn Creek
by boat by 9 AM. There they wait, gnashing their
teeth at the delays, till the helicopter finally whop-
whops down about 12:40 PM. They could have
walked back in by that time.

     The helicopter, new stuff in '49, is a small
Bell 47-D 2-seat whirlybird which even with the
roof-bubble off can carry only one passenger and
his tools---or one body in a stokes litter lashed to
the side---at a time. Because Dodge can see how
frustrated Ranger Jansson is, he lets him be the
first passenger on its many-trip shuttle to a high
flat right at the top of Mann Gulch. Jansson lands
at the pass about 1 PM and immediately starts
back to where they had found the first three
bodies earlier that morning.

For the rest of the afternoon Ranger Robert Jansson, who hasn't slept or quit working in almost 36 hours, finds and tries to identify six more bodies. He finally can't stand to go down and look at the crumbled remains of body #10 and plods on down Mann Gulch to its mouth where he meets Dr. Little and Wag Dodge. They hail a boat at about 6 PM and head back to Meriwether.

The next day the same crew, still led by Homer "Skip" Stratton, one of those experienced squadleaders who jumped in Washington with Bill Hellman, locates, gathers up and identifies the last two bodies. And the death toll of the Mann Gulch Fire rises to its final count: thirteen.

Earl Cooley tells the rest of the fire's story in two succinct paragraphs in <u>Trimotor and Trail</u>:

It took a massive effort to corral this killer fire. The U.S. Air Force base in Spokane contributed five transport planes. Two hundred trained firefighters were called from Lewiston, Coeur d'Alene, and Moscow, Idaho, and flown to Helena. Firefighters were recruited at Helena and were trucked in from other points. Farmers and ranchers volunteered. The U.S. Reclamation Service, Montana State Highway Patrol, and the U.S. Air Force base at Great Falls, Montana, sent men to lend a hand. Virtually every national forest in western Montana contributed firefighters and experienced supervisory personnel. A ten-mule packstring was trucked in from the Forest Service Remount Depot near Missoula. Eventually five fire camps ringed the Mann Gulch fire: Meriwether Canyon, Elkhorn Gulch, Willow Creek, Kennedy

Springs, and Willow Mountain. A total of 450 men worked on the fire. The camps communicated by radio. The State of Montana, the Montana Power Company, and the Forest Service supplied the radio facilities.

With the aid of a light rain, the spread of the Mann Gulch fire was stopped on Sunday, August 7. The fire was surrounded by fire-line on August 10, five days after the start. The burned area totaled an estimated 5,000 acres.

[End of Cooley quote.]

Years later a bronze plaque went up at Meriwether Campground:

IN MEMORY OF
the 13 heroic young men who lost their lives in the service of their country fighting the Mann Gulch forest fire 1 mile down the river on
August 5, 1949

ROBERT J. BENNETT [22 '51]   Paris, Tennessee
ELDON E. DIETTERT [19 '52] Missoula, Montana
JAMES O. HARRISON [20 '50] Missoula, Montana
WILLIAM J. HELLMAN [24 '50] Kalispell, Montana
PHILIP McVEY   [22 '51]   Ronan, Montana
DAVID R. NAVON [28]   Modesto, California
LEONARD L. PIPER [23 '51]   Blairsville, Pa.
STANLEY J. REBA [25]   Brooklyn, New York
MARVIN L. SHERMAN [21]   Missoula, Montana
JOSEPH B. SYLVIA [24] Plymouth, Massachusetts
HENRY J. THOL, JR. [19]   Kalispell, Montana
NEWTON R. THOMPSON [23] Alhambra, California
SILAS R. THOMPSON [21 '50]   Charlotte, N. C.

Inserted here in brackets after each man's name is his age at death, followed by, in 7 cases, the year he expected to graduate from the University of Montana, Missoula. But they all were stopped forever in August '49.

Bill Hellman was only three months from completing his degree and his preparation to be a teacher of science and botany. (Teachers with their summers free can go on smokejumping you see.)

Mrs. Gerry Hellman of Kalispell not only lost her husband Bill in the Mann Gulch disaster, but three months later, in November, their baby son suffered a ruptured diaphragm and his breathing stopped. Her anguish was complete.

Stan Reba---the man who had broken his leg and burned to ashes in a clump of heavy fuel---had been married too. For less than a year, to a beautiful girl he had met at the University of Minnesota. And due to his required military training with his reserve officers' unit for the first six weeks of the summer, he and Joe Sylvia had arrived at Missoula quite late for their refresher jumps and re-training. In fact on Friday, July 29--- a week before Mann Gulch---as they left Minnesota after seeing his wife for the last time, his father-in-law, quite concerned, asked him about how dangerous is this parachuting on forest fires. And Stan Reba, Air Corps veteran, first lieutenant in the Army Reserve and a second year smokejumper, answered that they should not worry about him, because it was quite safe and he would be okay.

His beautiful wife grieved for him, and never remarried, and ten years later took her own life.

Letter on Mann Gulch

Tuesday, August 9, 1949
Parachute Loft, Missoula

Dear Folks,

Well, I imagine you've read all about our tragedy. At least it was written up big in the local papers. Twelve of our 150 man crew were burned to death (along with one ground man) on the Helena National Forest last Friday afternoon. Their deaths had nothing to do with jumping, as they all landed safely and were out of their gear when it happened. They had jumped (fifteen of them) on the fire when it was 125 acres [later reported to be only sixty acres]---much bigger than the normal smokejumper situation---and the men were moving along a steep grassy slope on the opposite side of a draw from the fire when a sudden change of wind (at high velocity) trapped them. The temperature was 102 degrees outside the imme-diate fire area, so you can imagine how that grass exploded into flame.

The foreman, a fine guy named Wag Dodge, told them to stay with him while he burned out an area in the slope ahead of the uprushing line of flame to furnish them all a fuel-less safety area. This was exactly the right thing to do. He lit the grass with one match, and the heat and wind burned a half-acre patch in thirty seconds; but one man, seeing the wall of flame surging up toward them, shouted, "To hell with that! I'm getting out of here!" and broke and ran in panic. Everybody ran then but Wag Dodge. He lay down in the center of the tiny burned area [which was getting bigger above him every second], wet a handkerchief with his canteen and put it over his mouth, and pressed his face flat in the dirt. The fire roared over him without burning him at all. Of the other fourteen [plus one ground firefighter], two succeeded in topping the ridge and finding a barren rockslide to huddle in and were also unharmed. Two more were found alive (one a mere thirty yards behind the lucky first two) but both died of their burns in the hospital the next day. The other ten [plus the ground man] were killed outright by the blasting heat as they ran and a few of their bodies burned to unrecognizable rubble. All of which is a horrible example of the difference between panic and cool-headedness.

Among the twelve was my good friend Dave Navon, the 28-year-old ex-paratrooper and forestry graduate from Cal---the guy I described in one of the letters. He'd studied at the University of Aberdeen in Scotland last year. A wonderful guy and good friend. It's hard to believe he won't be around any more. I got a letter from him a week ago today. And to deal another death blow to the stupidity of anti-Semitism (like that felt by Leo Kelmenson), Dave is having a service at a synagogue in San Francisco before burial near home.

Three others of the twelve were among our thirteen men up at Sullivan Lake for three-and-a-half weeks, Hank Thol, Lenny Piper and Bob Bennett, and they flew back with us to Missoula last Tuesday evening. We worked Wednesday morning at the loft (when incidentally Don Hoover, my '47 Blister Rust buddy, called up and we arranged to meet that night), but a fire call came in from Yellowstone Park that afternoon for eight men and I was on it. Consequently Hoover, who was broke, jobless and apparently not wheat harvesting, didn't get to see me, and we didn't have a chance to talk over old times.

It's a long flight in the Ford Trimotor to where we jumped in south Yellowstone (2 PM to 4 PM plus a half-hour stop at West Yellowstone), and we jumped around 5---two at a time on small fires out in the mountains. Great fun and meaty overtime. We didn't hear the sad news till Cole (my partner) and I arrived back in Missoula by train Saturday afternoon.

Hughie made another jump up in the St. Joe National Forest over the weekend and got back this morning. He's all okay and had a good fire, but he too was shocked to find out the terrible news about our lost twelve. And he missed going on it by eight or so on the other side of the jump list himself.

It's a hot week and we expect more action tomorrow.

Leo Kelmenson has invited me on either a sailing race (Providence to Nova Scotia) or a cruise (Block Island, Nantucket, Cape Cod) on his 36-foot sloop, <u>The Bunny</u>, depending on if the race comes off or not, the first two weeks of September. I'm all hopped up about it and have accepted. I'll fly back---coach fare to New York is only about $80. It will take most of the savings again, but what the hell---you only live once. Anyway if I don't take an ocean cruise-sailing this time, I may never get another chance.

Yours for bigger and bluer horizons.

Love,

Starr

Lewis and Clark Fire

The Lewis and Clark National Forest is made of six scattered pieces of mountain-range forest land stretching from about the center of Montana up to just below Glacier National Park. The biggest piece of the Lewis and Clark is that l00 mile strip which occupies the eastern slope of the Continental Divide as she emerges from Glacier Park and winds her way south to near Lewis and Clark Pass just north of the Helena. This is the east slope of the main range of the Northern Rocky Mountains and includes the Sun River Primitive Area and big mountains of sharp gray flint emerging out of scraggly pine and fir forests. To the west is the much broader strip of the Flathead National Forest including the Bob Marshall Wilderness Area. To the south is the Helena National Forest. And to the east is the Great Plains starting with part of the Blackfeet Indian Reservation and the country around the town of Choteau and the city of Great Falls.

It was to a fire in the Sun River Primitive
Area that a Ford load of eight jumpers was called
out the Sunday morning of August 14. The fire
was due northeast of Missoula about 80 miles and
due west of Great Falls about the same distance.
The fire was five acres and spreading fast when
the jumpers came over and stepped out; and the
first eight ground men, hiking up from below, also
arrived about the same time. The ground men of
course had been slogging uphill with full packs and
tools since 4 AM to get there and were understandably bushed. The sixteen men together could
not hold it, and it was soon apparent that the
number of men jumped in should have been 24 or
32, or maybe 48, because it takes fresh tough
men to build fireline fast in steep mountains of flint
and forest.

I was in the second (and last) batch of eight
jumpers who sailed down to fight it in the afternoon, also out of a roaring Ford; and the Lewis and
Clark Forest also poured in a total of 150 ground
pounders including the regular district fire-
suppression men, a crew of Houderites (a bearded
sect like the Mennonites who are good firefighters), soldiers, and a collection of rummies from the
bars of Great Falls.

Of all these we smokejumpers thought we
did by far the best and the most work. But that is
as it should be---for we are certainly the Forest
Service's shock troops in that part of the world.
To testify to this fact, I heard the fireboss, in
calling out for more men on the radio, ask his
headquarters for "twenty-five more jumpers, or if
they aren't available, fifty more ground men."

It was spectacular lonesome country: huge mountains of sharp bladey flint with timber scraggling up the sides, glacier-gouged valleys and ridges, all out where <u>everything</u> to support man had to come in by air or pack-mule.

The fire kept spreading fast in spite of all we could do, and the now large crew was divided into day and night shifts of twelve hours each, and my group was put on the night shift right after supper. With all those separate groups, as you might well imagine, we had a very disorganized fire camp at first, straightening out later but with consistently lousy food.

That food quality may have been because the fireboss tried to keep as many as possible of the bar flies from Great Falls on the mess-tent detail (and of course most of the bar flies wanted that too) so that they wouldn't be out killing each other with sharp axes and shovels trying to cut fireline.

The fire continued to spread Sunday night, and all day Monday, until it reached about 160 acres, if you were looking down on a flat map and considered the land to all be level too. We figured it to be about 300 acres if you could accurately measure all those ups and downs. [As Jock Hendrickson remarked one time, "If you took all the mountains in Western Montana and pounded 'em down flat, they'd cover the whole Newnited States!"] Steep rocky terrain, slidy, with lots of falling snags (more dangerous than jumping), but good weather for living in the open. We got it controlled Tuesday and spent the next two nights and a day mopping it up.

The first group of eight jumpers was on the day shift, and my eight-man crew was on the night shift four nights in a row. As such we saw some gorgeous if terrible scenes of whole trees flaming up in the night. But luckily no crown fire developed. Thank God there was no big wind that night.

This was the fire on which I messed myself up as a firefighter in the most serious way---by deserting my post on the fireline---to <u>sleep</u> a little ways back in the forest for a couple of hours during the long cool night---and being missed by the smokejumper foreman as he came along the line checking up on his men and his section of the fire-perimeter. This offense was not quite enough to get me fired on the spot---since the burn was quiet just then and no harm was done---but it was enough to cause me not to be rehired the following summer---a grievous punishment to any smoke-jumper who wants to come back.

My rationalization for doing this rotten deed---especially rotten after Mann Gulch---was unpersuasive. But it went like this: Having worked fighting fire in California (Region 5 of the U.S. Forest Service) and in Oregon (part of Region 6), I had the mistaken illusion that it was quite legal and proper to take two hours of sleep out of every 24 if the fire in your sector was quiet and not flaring up and if you really needed the sleep. [This illusion was probably my own misreading of a custom that held true in some firefighting situations as far as timekeeping and pay were concerned: That is, that if a firefighter out on his own (but not on a crew) reported that he had worked straight through for 24 hours (a frequent occurrence), the paymaster would only pay him for 22 of those hours, considering that he must have spent at least two of those 24 hours eating to keep himself fueled for all that hard work. And they weren't going to pay you for four lunch half-hours.] Holding this misconception, I thought I had tacit permission to grab two hours sleep when my sector of the fireline was quiet. And I considered my mental alarm system, to wake me up in just two hours, to be reliable. But having trained in California, I was also concerned about the dangers of snags falling on you---the dead tree, the one most likely to have been hit by lightning, that has burned through at the butt and that now comes falling, perhaps silently, out of the night sky to crush you. I'd heard once that more firefighters were killed by falling snags than by the fires themselves, so I always wanted to be alert or out of reach on that score. [They say when you hear a tree cracking and starting to come down, you should not just run blindly away but should look up and try to see which way it's going (or coming) so you can perhaps leap in the right direction to avoid that fatal blow.]

Since we had seen many a snag and tree already fall in this fire, I decided to move back from the line for my "legal" two-hour nap. I picked a U-shaped part of the line (the smoldering burn on the outside of the U) and went to the center of the U to stretch out, a spot I thought would be out of reach of most falling snags but from which I could hear any flareups of the fire that might occur in the area. And that's where I was snoring when the

foreman came by patrolling the trail and didn't find
me. But he found the empty space on the trail.
        Two very serious violations:
                Desertion of post.
                And sleeping on duty.
        His seasonal personnel rating will be
unsatisfactory to say the least. [You've done it
again, Jenkins.]   But right now we have a hot fire
season going, and he's a hell of a lot better than
these drunks from Great Falls.

        I guess I just answered the question of
whether or not I would have run at Mann Gulch.

        And on that Friday night of August 5, nine
to midnight, while Joe Sylvia and Bill Hellman (5
weeks a father) clung to life on their rock slabs,
mortally burned and dying of thirst, I was coming
off my Yellowstone fire with white-muddied boots
at a <u>dance</u> in Mammoth Village---and was jiving
with a beautiful black-haired telephone operator
from Provo, Utah.

        By Thursday morning we had mopped up
the fire enough for the main fireboss to start
releasing crews. The drunks first (fairly sober and
getting healthy by now) to get them off this
mountain before they kill themselves or somebody
else with a pulaski. Then the smokejumpers so
they can be ready to hit somewhere else fast.
I wish we had hit this one with 32 of 'em last
Sunday morning.
        "Okay Jumpers, leave all your gear in
labeled sacks near the packer corral downstream

of the mess-tent. A pack-string of mules will carry
out your heavy gear to the trucks at the road-head.
And thanks, men, for a job well done."
    [All but one.]

                *   *   *

    Despite our filth and whiskers, soon we
were enjoying getting paid to hike downhill without
a pack out of the Sun River Primitive Area, out of
the high flinty mountains where any rock was a
sword into the thicker forest with open grassy
slopes here and there, keeping our eyes peeled for
bighorn sheep and grizzly bear. Sun River country,
as beautiful as you'll find anywhere.
    The trail ran alongside tumbling streams,
flowing down to form Sun River itself, which went
tumbling farther down into foothills and then into
the Great Plains and on to the Missouri. About
halfway down we got to the road-head and had a
nice open-air truck-ride to the ranger station at
Choteau and spent a half-day there cleaning up,
gorging on free steaks and catching up on our
sleep. Yes, I still needed some.
    In late afternoon they took us to the airport
where the Doug was just landing. And we had a
beautiful open-door flight back over the Divide to
Missoula as the sun was setting.   Wonderful life!

Letter from Hugh

Parachute Loft, Missoula
Tuesday, August 16, 1949

Dear Folks,

Here I am at the Loft again, waiting for
another fire jump. Starr was sent on a fire a
couple of days ago and hasn't gotten back yet.
They sent eight men out this afternoon, so I'm
about fifteenth on the old list.

Today another fellow and I worked out at
the radio station, which is situated on one of the
bare slopes which overlook Missoula and the
airport. The radio station is a neat little white
building belonging to the Forest Service, which
handles all the radio work of Region One. Our job
was just to saw up some old fifteen-inch poles and
split them into firewood. My associate was Bob
Holmstrom, who was on the Avery fire with me
and is a law student at Montana State. We
worked all day under the sun without shirts, and
got toasted a deep red-brown. I liked the job---and
learning how to handle a crosscut is really worth-
while. Every bit of experience helps. I've had just

a smattering of saw and axe work this summer, and have gained a great respect for the tools themselves---and those who can use them.

Both of them are real precision instruments, extremely simple and yet extremely complex--- products of centuries of evolution, not to mention the craftsmanship and high-quality material that goes into them. A good sharp flexible six-foot crosscut seems to cut with a will of its own. All the sawyers are supposed to do is to whip it back and forth with a slight rocking motion in the easiest, lightest, most delicate manner possible. The only downward weight is the weight of the blade itself. For a tool which is entirely manually operated, it's a miracle. In the same way, a good sharp axe bites deeper into the wood than you'd believe. An axe-handle is a masterpiece in itself; smooth, balanced, fitted so closely to the head and so strong that it stands thousands of chopping strokes without loosening or breaking.

Am reading Wolfe's <u>Look Homeward</u>, <u>Angel</u>, and adore it. For all its ragged, jagged edges, it makes more ordinary masterpieces seem strained and affected. Critics who scorn purplish prose seem foolish to me. Why not make full use of the language you're using? Yep, after I get out of Oberlin I'll have to write a novel.

Love,

Hugh

Double Delight in the Bitterroot Wilderness
(Letter from Starr)

Parachute Loft, USFS, Missoula, Montana
Wednesday, August 24, '49

Dear Folks,

What a week! Two fires; 29 hours of
overtime; two wires from Leo (which I did not get
until today) as to whether I'm coming on the cruise
or not; a lot of flying in and out of all kinds of little
airstrips buried in the rugged canyons and
mountains of northern Idaho, in a Ford Trimotor
and a Bell 47-D helicopter.

Incidentally, thanks <u>mucho</u> for the bail-out
check received today. I shall repay! I am still
going east, leaving by commercial airliner (small
size) Friday night; into New York City Saturday
afternoon; starting the cruise out of Manhasset
Bay, Long Island, Sunday morning.

This latest double whammy smokejumper
adventure started <u>early</u> last Sunday morning. I
was getting back to the barracks about 2 AM after
a Saturday night of pursuing nurses and coeds,

when I saw, thoughtfully posted above the urinals, a notice calling for me and Frank Dotz to be up by 4 AM to be ready, all suited-up, for takeoff at 5! Frank is a rangy first-year jumper who wears logger's clothes but has a cowboy's lantern jaw. Several of us were being called out to cover several small 2-man lightning-fires down in the Bitterroot National Forest in the Selway-Bitterroot Wilderness. I got my two hours of sleep, staggered out of the sack at 4, got ready while wolfing down a few rations for breakfast, and droned aloft as scheduled.

We turned southwest in the pale light, flew over shadowy canyons beneath the sunny tip of Lolo Peak. Soon we were over the trail now a road which Lewis and Clark used to fight their way back over the snow-covered Bitterroot Mountains in 1806, and we topped the divide into Idaho.

It was a rough fire to find that early in the morning. When fires have been started by night-lightning, many don't even show at all till eleven o'clock in the morning or even a week later. A few that are burning hotter will sometimes loft a thin column of pale smoke straight up into the still air for about 15 minutes after first light. Then the warming air will generate winds and the smoke will be blown away and the fire may remain invisible till noon or afternoon or a week later. [That's why we were out there, trying to be there for that magic first fifteen minutes.] Yet as we were over the general area of the fire about 5:35 no smoke could we see.

The spotter then realized that, since our radio was not switchable to the same frequency of

all of the 16 Region One national forests (each one
being different), we were going to have to buzz a
nearby lookout tower to wake up the lookout to
get a signal-of-bearing streamer laid out on the
ground pointing to this fire. The spotter conveyed
this to the pilot with a few cryptic hand signals
and the cheery words, "Well, Slim, I guess we
better wake 'em up."

Slim Phillips, the pilot, gleefully throttled
down into a quiet glide, and the old bird sifted
down into the valley below the lookout, and then
climbed sneakily up the timbered slope about 100
feet above the trees. [This was Slim Phillips flying,
the Johnson Flying Service pilot who, it was
rumored, had once taken up a Ford Trimotor
ostensibly to test a new radio and had flown the
old Tin Goose out of sight of Missoula and dived
her down into a faraway canyon and pulled her
back up, and up, and up, until he put her into and
over and through a complete loop! It was said that
Slim afterwards reported that the new radio had
worked perfectly. It was further reported that he
had had an unnamed fellow pilot along---each of
them wearing flatpack chutes---so that he could
have a witness and a signed affidavit to the fact
that a Ford Trimotor built in 1927 could indeed
survive a loop in 1947---or whenever it was. And
that they had sent said signed and witnessed
affidavit to the Ford Motor Company, and that
Henry Ford II himself personally, but secretly, sent
each of them a brand new Thunderbird for their
pains. Come to think of it, Thunderbird is the
perfect name for a Ford Trimotor yet.]

As the Trimotor sprang over the edge of the

forest at the slumbering lookout tower, Slim had all
three throttles on full power. And with three
uncowled radial engines crashing their loudest, the
square-cut dragon roared by the tower some fifty
feet out from its southeast balcony. Slim snarled
his throttles and rolled the lookout couple out of
bed with a tremendous crescendo of noise. Then
we swung back by and the spotter dropped a
signal streamer with note to the quaking couple
fleeing down the ladder in their night clothes.

"Aw shucks. They had their jammies on,"
roared Phillips.

Then the spotter took the sting out of all
this by throwing out another drift-chute upon the
tower-clearing below. Swinging beneath that
miniature chute were a sack of fresh apples and a
rolled-up copy of today's Sunday Morning
Missoulian. So that sucker had planned this
torture all along.

When the lookout-husband finally got the
signal streamer lined up, Slim followed the arrow
straight over three ridges and there---a third of the
way down a long slope of white pine---was the
little fire showing just a wisp of blue smoke
against the dark trees. We could even see a tiny
line of flame eating its way through the duff.

Because there were a lot of snags and rocks
close around the fire, the spotter decided that a
little meadow near the ridge about a mile and a
half from the fire was the safest place to put us
down. (They're real careful since the disaster at
Mann Gulch.) And a gentle wind was now
blowing cross-ways to the ridge, so he had me and
Frank step out 200 yards upwind of that ridge one

at a time. It was lovely coming down over those
wrinkled ridges in the dewy morning, trying to hit
that meadow.

We landed okay, sacked up our suits, hiked
the mile and a half to the fire while watching them
drop our cargo in in good shape. The fire was
about one-eighth of an acre and we spent a
vigorous day wrapping it up. Since the country
was cool and moist, we decided we could start to
leave that dead burn that evening. It was a terrific
drag up a long rockslide with all our tools, chow,
bedrolls, utensils and cargo chutes to the ridge
where our jump gear was waiting.

We got there about midnight. Seeing no fire
then below, and smelling no smoke, we slept till 5
AM, got up to have breakfast, checked the fire
again, and later met the mule packer who had
come out eleven miles from Moose Creek Ranger
Station to pack all our gear back in. While he
undertook the precision job of packing our gear on
his mules, we strolled on in, carrying only lunch
and canteens, grateful to be relieved of those
burdens, enjoying a hike through the wilderness on
Uncle Sam's payroll.

Our hike-out was a breeze, mostly along
ridge-trails, downhill and often alongside tumbling
clear streams. Coming down a canyon we
encountered a homesteader cabin on a little chip of
private land within the forest. The teenage cabin-
wife affirmed that yes, this was the trail to Moose
Creek (since we were already off our scrap of map
as usual). She also seemed so glad to see
anybody who was alive and breathing (even as
filthy as we were) that she fired up the woodstove

and soon spread before us a feast of bacon, eggs,
biscuits, steaks, potatoes, gravy, carrots, apple pie
and coffee for our lunch. We ate it all with gusto.
[Hmm. Great steaks. A little wild maybe.
Definitely not beef.] In gratitude we left her the
chocolate bars and cans of fruit we were carrying,
forged on ahead, and soon came out into a
beautiful river valley with a clump of log buildings,
corrals, pack-mules and an airstrip. Ah, this must
be the ranger station. But that's funny. No
familiar pine-tree sign out front. We strolled into
the main log building---rather sumptuous for the
Forest Service---looking for someone to report to.
Nobody at home at the open front desk. There on
the wall was a large map of the Selway-Bitterroot
Wilderness Area. Frank was looking around to find
someone while I studied the map.

"Hey Frank! This is not Moose Creek
Ranger Station."

"It ain't? Then what is it?"

"It must be a dude ranch or lodge or
somethin'. Moose Creek R.S. looks to be about
four miles downstream by the lay of this map."

"Okay. Best we get out of here."

Outside along the stream---a creek with
more water in it than the Rio Grande has at
Albuquerque---we soon saw a fly-fisherman
wading in the stream, his graceful line flicking out
over the water. He stopped to talk and it turned
out he had flown in from Chicago by private plane
a couple of days before. [Fly-fisherman; get it?]
But he knew enough about the place to confirm
our find. So we swallowed our embarrassment as
woodsmen who did not know the country and

strolled downstream to our day's-end goal.

Moose Creek Ranger Station is a tiny oasis of civilization in a vast desert of timber and mountains. And the civilization is mostly 19th century---mules, corrals, log cabins, blacksmith shop---with a few 20th century touches---an airstrip, radios, and this summer only, a new Bell helicopter being tested as a wilderness firefighting system. Moose Creek is in the heart of the rugged Bitterroots, reachable only by plane or pack-mule---or by hiking or riding a horse 25 miles, up over a 6500 foot divide, from the nearest road over in Montana. The only "settlements" in here (either Forest Service establishments or a few homesteader ranches made into dude ranches for fly-in dudes) have their own small airstrips---or they don't get much outside contact.

We rested at Moose Creek Ranger Station that night and part of a day, waiting for the Ford to come in and take us out. Four jumpers were in there on project, working on the helicopter experiment---clearing small landing spots on strategic knobs throughout the district so it could be covered adequately for fire by copter. While we were there that night a second lightning storm set several more small fires, and when daylight came here was a perfect chance to test in action the new helicopter method. The lookouts were calling in with the coordinates of the strikes that took fire; and as soon as the rain stopped, the "infuriated palm tree," as Bob Johnson called it, began shuttling out with one firefighter at a time to take care of the fires as speedily as possible. Mike Hardy was using his crew in close cooperation with the Moose Creek District Ranger.

Smokejumper Jake Dougherty took one small fire by himself, as did Herb Oertli. That left one other burning in the district that would probably take two men to handle by the time it could be reached. The other two men in the jumper labor crew who had worked all summer with this machine were Frank Anywaush and Ed Ladendorff. Certainly they ought to go. But Frank had a sprained shoulder and was waiting with us to go out in the Ford. So, I got the job of going with Ladendorff on the remaining two-man fire.

Mike Hardy explained the method to us. The copter would take us ten miles down the canyon to Bear Creek Fork, fly us up and show us the fire, which was five miles uphill from where we could be landed, and then go back down and let us out in the Bear Creek meadow. We were to cross the bridge, hike up a trail with our firepacks on our backs, and arrive at the fire well before sundown if all went well. The copter would be back over at that time to drop us bedrolls and extra supplies.

Strapped in beside Pilot Happy Jack Hughes, Ed Ladendorff took off first, his left arm curled around a clackboard-mounted firepack that contained K-rations, fire tools, flashlight, map case and canteen. The helicopter flailed itself off the ground, turned to climb steeply away over the Moose Creek strip, and soon disappeared down the canyon. And I got my fire clothes back on ready to go.

Half an hour later the copter was back, and it was my turn to make my way toward Bear Creek Fork. The Bell 47-D with its bubble canopy off is a mighty open-air affair. No doors, no roof; just a windshield in front that goes all the way down to your feet. And you are sitting there in the sky with nothing to hold you there but one strap across your middle. Then you and the pilot more or less drive through the air. I feel much safer at low altitude in a copter than in a plane.

Hughes took me over Bear Creek and up over the fire so I would get the lay of the land for finding my way up; and we came back to the meadow low, following the Crow Creek trail down as far as we could through the woods before losing it. Ladendorff was waiting for me at the meadow, and we both shouldered our packs and started up.

Two hours and 5 miles later, after much puffing and climbing and verbal reflections on the advantages of jumping into fires rather than ground-pounding our way up to them, we arrived on the scene---4 hours from the time of the report. Then the helicopter was back with Hardy in the cargo-dropper's spot, and they bulls-eyed us from 150 feet with a sack that contained two goose-down bedrolls, some fresh sandwiches and chocolate bars (sparing us from the K-rations for a while), and two cans of cold beer. Helicopters are wonderful!

The fire was almost a model of two-man size, about 300 square feet, burning quietly through open, brush-free duff on the top of a beautiful ponderosa-covered ridge. We had it trailed and mopped up by 10 o'clock that night, and then sat till midnight, watching the cold of the night kill off the last of the embers.

After 5 hours of sleep on the goose-downs, we were up at 5 for the final hand-check of the burn. The fire was good and dead. We had accomplished our mission some 18 hours after the lightning had struck. We packed our stuff (no jump suits or chutes this time) and hiked back down to Bear Creek Cabin, near the meadow below.

Phoned in to Moose Creek and they told us to walk downstream two miles to Shearer Airstrip for lunch and to catch the Ford Trimotor which was due to fly down there shortly. The Ford had just flown in four drums of gasoline for the helicopter at Moose Creek, then was coming down here empty to Shearer for us. That made us feel pretty good. And we started on down.

After lunch on the outdoor terrace at Shearer International Airport---a single strip of clearing in the forest about a quarter mile long, rolling through a bow-shaped canyon-bottom---we soon heard a drone. Then that humorous old plane crept in over the ridge to our north, a few feet above the treetops, banked in one way and sideslipped the other, all of which were necessary to get it into that tiny rolling strip in the canyon-bottom. The pilot touched down, rolled the plane clear up to the trees on the uphill end, spun the plane around and locked his brakes till we got aboard. "Get you and your gear forward, guys, and hang on!" Then he gunned her downhill, across the flat and lifted her out of there (she takes off at 55), roaring her back up the canyon, topping the ridge-spurs by anything from 200 to 500 feet, back to Moose Creek.

That Ford is some airplane. Ancient as she
is, she will do things no other plane can. But it
takes a real mountain pilot, preferably one who
knows the country, to drive her too.

The Moose Creek airstrip is longer and wider
than most of these canyon-bottom strips. It's cut
out of the forest to a length that will accommodate
even the Douglas DC-3. In fact it is wide enough
in one spot that once, in a 40 mph cross-wind, a
Ford Trimotor with a full load of jumpers took off
<u>crossways</u> to that main airstrip. With that kind of
a headwind the old Ford was able to take off with
about a l5 mph ground speed at full throttle.

Also to get in there you fly over Moose
Creek fairly low, fly down the canyon losing
altitude until you get to a wide bowl in the
mountains where the creek makes a U-turn. Then
you go around the bowl with your wingtips almost
scraping the trees. Then, going in the reverse
direction, you drop down the rest of the way to
the upper end of the strip. And keep a sharp eye
out for deer on the "runway."

Landed at Moose Creek, dropped off Ed and
the firetools and took on Frank Dotz and the other
injured smokejumper, the empty gas drums and our
jump gear, and flew back over the Bitterroots to
Missoula.

End of my last fires for the season.

Have been in a big storm getting ready to
depart (they'd like you to stay through at least
Labor Day after all this training), but the sea is
calling and I've got to go. Besides, the end of a
fire season, with the rain falling and a steadily

dwindling crew, is a time for the bad, bad blues. Might as well be one of the first to quit---especially for such a privilege as to become a crewman on an ocean-going sloop, sailing around Long Island and Nantucket.

Things are finally all shaping up for a tomorrow afternoon termination. Yet it's something I really hate to do---ever to quit being a smokejumper. For I know that ever being one is inoculating yourself with a deadly disease: The fever in the blood that will return every spring, and smolder every June, and leap into flame every July, and rage into an inferno every August. The rage to be forever one of the brothers in the sky.

But after tomorrow it will all be over. At least for this year.

Or maybe forever.

By now you may have seen the most recent issue of LIFE (August 22, 1949)---the one with its leading news-story (with Peter Stackpole photos) being, "Smokejumpers Suffer Ordeal by Fire" on the Mann Gulch disaster---which killed twelve of our best. My first time ever to get into LIFE---and I'm not enthused about it at all.

*   *   *

Some pictures, packages and maps will be coming your way from me, Mom. Open them if you like.

Love you.

Thanks for everything.

Starr

Two Notes on a Dying Fire Season
(from Hugh)

Dear Folks,

Another two weeks and my summer will be
over. Rain and cold have been closing in this
weekend, and there may be no more fires this
year. I can be satisfied with the season, though.
Have made plenty of overtime this year, although
getting fewer jumps than some of the other guys.
And this job, in spite of the occasional monotony,
pettiness and filth, has plenty of splendid
moments. Flying low over mountains is always
unbelievably exciting to me, seeing the completely
patternless, jumbled topography of Montana and
Idaho from the air, with so many ragged peaks and
shadowed canyons stretching everywhere to the
horizon.

Firefighting is wretched work, but jumping
has my interest more than ever. Now that I've had
enough experience to feel I can handle any chute

maladjustments which might possibly develop, I
can get real enjoyment out of a jump---standing in
the door with the terrific wind in the face, and
then stepping out into that moving air---the
sensation of falling and then the opening shock,
and the easy sliding down to earth. Wonderful!

I just finished reading The Oregon Trail
which Starr gave me last spring as a birthday
present, along with the Rommel book. It certainly
is great to get a truly contemporary account of the
1846 migrations, the Oregon-bound Missourians,
the Sioux and buffalo and mountain men, Fort
Laramie, etc. I can find plenty of faults with
Parkman though---aside from his frequent bad
writing. His Brahmin contempt for the westerners
and Indians is something galling. I can imagine
what a pain this twenty-three-year-old Boston
aristocrat was to the guides and helpers he hired
for the trip. It is interesting to see how much
Parkman and Dana had in common. Did Two
Years Before the Mast come out before or after
The Oregon Trail?

I get kind of a kick out of thinking of the
two upper-class young men adventuring in the
world of ordinary people and returning to write
books about their experiences for their family and
friends. Well, I shouldn't be too hard on them,
because I may write a book myself someday.
Seven Seasons Among the Montana FireDevils, by
H. Jenkins. Violence and color on every page . . .

Love,
Hugh

Another note to Starr:

We've had rain and cold these past few days, and it looks like the fire season has come to a premature end. The breeze has that September chill in it, and the end-of-season blues are hanging heavy over the whole outfit. A few of the guys have terminated, and the yearly disintegration of the outfit has begun. This particular group, the hundred-and-fifty-odd men who made up the 1949 Region One smokejumping crew, will be disbanded and dead in a few more days. Both the chicken-shit and the glory will be past, reliving only in an occasional memory. Times like these bring out the meditative in me . . . .

The boys who flew over to Grants Pass, Oregon, haven't returned yet, and exactly what they are doing is uncertain. By the way, that fellow Nolan you worked with at Cave Junction passed through the other day. He took first place in that jump contest at the National Air Races at Detroit, and won a couple of thousand dollars. He was travelling with George Harpole, who took fourth; and we shook hands. There were five slotted chutes among the twenty competing, but Nolan and Harpole were the only smokejumpers, and only their slots did any good . . . .

Well, Starr, best of luck on your great trip east. Be seeing you soon.

Regards; your bro,
Hugh

Go East Young Man

Main Airport   Friday Evening
Missoula, Montana   August 26, 1949
          The plane taxiing up to the air terminal was
a twin-engined propeller-driven Martin 202, riding
high and level on its new-fangled tricycle landing
gear. Northwest Airlines, just in from Seattle and
Spokane, en route to Minneapolis and Chicago. (In
Chicago I was to change planes for Idyllwilde
Airport, New York, there to meet Leo and start on
that great sail---if the hurricane season didn't wipe
us out.)
          This plane looked new, sturdy and business-
like compared to the old craft I had been thrashing
about in all summer. The pilot followed his
signalman to his marks on the tarmac, snarled the
plane to just the right spot, cut the engines to
propeller-stop, and lowered the rectal part of the
fuselage to the ground as a rear-facing stairway.
"Hey, it carries its own ladder." Rightly so in little
airports in the Northwest.

A few people got off and a few got on, and as we newcomers settled into our seats I was still wearing the uniform of the day: clean work shirt, clean blue jeans, gray-green whipcord timber-cruiser's jacket with all those pockets, and paratrooper boots with the white mud of Yellowstone long since cleaned off them. I was naturally reluctant to give them up and was hoping someone might ask, "Why the boots?"

But despite the previous pangs of leaving my buddies in parachute firefighting, it felt good to be on the way at last. The airline stewardess in her cute outfit was checking to see if everyone had fastened his or her seatbelt.

"Seatbelts!" I said to myself without saying anything aloud. "Seatbelts!" Thinking of all the careening rides in the open backs of stakeside trucks over corduroy gravel roads above thousand-foot drop-offs. Of flights in the Doug with the door off and a safety strap hanging limp across the open space. Of sitting on a wooden bench in the Nasty Noorduyn with a static line in my hand. Of standing up in the curving door of the Doug so wind of the prop-blast tore at my facemask. To myself I said, "I just flew out of Moose Creek, Idaho, sitting on empty gasoline drums in the back of a Trimotor Ford, and you want me to put on a seatbelt?"

And then she looked at me sitting there grinning in that seat, and she smiled. And of course I fastened that seatbelt. And rejoined this modern, hopeful, tied-down world of 1949.

E P I L O G

Starr, despite all his efforts, didn't get rehired by the smokejumpers in 1950. His last parachute jump (his 18th) was a free-fall in June into Glen Canyon of the Colorado River (where Lake Powell now is). This jump was organized and led by a fellow Missoula jumper named Dave Burt. Dave, a rigger for the Missoula loft, a free-fall parachute jumper, and a geology major at the University of New Mexico, wanted a friend to help him make that trek. He wanted to fly with another pilot-friend out of Marble Canyon, Arizona, drop a small inflatable boat by cargo-chute onto a projecting sandbar, and, after returning to the airstrip for his chutes, fly back and leap in after it. The second member of the expedition would then come in on a third trip for the little Cessna across that maze of canyons and mesas. Then, after dropping drift chutes to assess the wind, he would jump in after Dave and the boat.

Dave, like Starr, thirsted to see wild country and to live great adventures. Dave knew all about free-fall parachuting. And Starr thought Dave needed a friend to help with the photography and the boat handling, not to mention general safety. The trip was suspense-filled, gritty, sweaty, almost scuttled by a 70-mile-an-hour sandstorm, but overall a great success. They got to see Rainbow Natural Bridge in its natural state (350 feet above its own private canyon), ancient Indian ruins still partially intact, and the roaring, muscular Colorado River coursing at 12 knots through its orange canyons in June. And they got spectacular slides of country now submerged under Lake Powell, never to be seen again.

As it turned out, that trip convinced Glen Ream, the principal of Albuquerque High, to hire Starr as a teacher in the fall---as someone who did things on his own that the kids would respect. (One of those kids, in 10th grade, was Bobby Unser, who later won fame by winning the Indy 500 several times.) It was Starr's first profess-ional job for the winter months. And a necessity for him to support his beautiful bride in their upcoming marriage.

Stella and Starr were married on August 14 (exactly one year after his jump on the Lewis and Clark fire); and they left immediately on a 12-day honeymoon to California. And the bride, like the Smokejumper Administration, was glad Starr was through with all that foolishness of firefighting and parachuting.

Hugh Jenkins, on the other hand, had two

more exciting seasons of smokejumping ('50 and '51), completing 22 jumps and achieving a good record. He graduated from Oberlin College in the class of '51. After the fire season and wangling a draft deferment as a conscientious objector, he started in briefly at UC Berkeley in history in the fall. Soon thereafter, however, realizing that the Korean War was an attempt by the U.S. and 16 other nations to build international law, he gave up being a conscientious objector. About that time, the CIA offered him a job, based on his parachute experience, as a "medical technician." The pay was to be a thousand dollars more a year than Starr was getting teaching school. And Hugh took it. And went back east for four months of intensive, secret training.

Eventually the draft board found out about this, canceled his deferment, and got him ousted from the CIA and ready to be drafted. In great despond at his shattered plans, Hugh went to see the just-released film, Red Skies of Montana, and cheered to see Richard Widmark snarling at his troops and the mass jump he, Hugh, was coming down in. He even spotted himself in another of the scenes for a few brief seconds.

Hugh then joined the Army, trained as an infantryman in South Carolina (they wouldn't even put him in the paratroopers after all this), and was sent across the country to his favorite place, San Francisco Bay. Soon he was on a troop transport crossing the Pacific to the Korean peninsula.

It was fall 1952, the stalemated third year of the Korean War, and Hugh was soon in the Fifteenth Infantry Regiment of the Third Division

doing trench warfare, with patrols ahead of the
Main Line of Resistance. The winter was fierce in
Korea. The troops had occasional skirmishes with
the North Koreans and the Chinese, with dead on
both sides showing that, though small in scale,
this was still very much a shooting war.

Finally the winter abated. Hugh and his
160-man company were assigned to defend the
hilltop "Outpost Harry" 400 yards ahead of the
MLR in the Chorwon Valley. At 2 AM on the
morning of April 25, 1953, a Chinese battalion of
750 men attacked. After a night of fierce fighting,
a quarter of the Chinese were killed and the rest
wounded or driven back. The Americans, though
suffering 16 killed and 66 wounded, held the hill.
Among the dead was Corporal Hugh Jenkins.

He was awarded the Silver Star for gallantry
in action that night as he helped hold his sector
together and tried to save the life of a wounded
buddy. And three months later the shooting
stopped.

Hugh's funeral was held in July in Chicago,
so he could be buried next to his World War I
veteran father who had died in 1942. Besides his
family, the only friend who came to Hugh's
funeral---700 miles from Washington, D.C.---was
Charles Reich.

Acknowledgments

Two of the chapters in this book are fiction, as specified below. In addition some of the dialogs in some of the remaining factual chapters are fictionalized though remaining true to the spirit of the situation as I understand it. Also I have taken the liberty of moving a few of Hugh's experiences from later smokejumper seasons back into the 1949 season to fairly represent his smokejumper life within the time frame of our title year.

The Charles to whom Hugh writes on occasion is Charles Reich, Hugh's former room-mate at Oberlin College and later the author of The Greening of America. Many thanks to Charles for permission to publish these letters.

The chief catalyst for generating this book is that Bay Area gentleman and great photographer, Peter Stackpole. Peter is the man whose splendid photographs grace these pages. Peter Stackpole of LIFE, of San Francisco Bay, of Hollywood, of Oakland, and now of Novato, California. An artist with a camera and a noble soul. Thank you, Peter, for capturing the jumpers of '49 and for wanting to bring out your '49 photos to reveal those smoke-jumpers to the world.

Grateful acknowledgments are here made to:

Laird Robinson for taking Bob Sallee, Hal Samsel, Short Hall and me on a very educational climb up through Mann Gulch.

Anita Navon and Jack Demmons for editorial help and suggestions.

The Saturday Evening Post for granting permission to republish "We Jump Into Fire," first published there April 28, 1951.

The publishers of <u>AIR BP</u> and <u>Book of Flight Today</u> for permission to reprint "The Greatest Thrill of Them All"---first published there in the summer 1960 issue.

<u>Short Stories</u> for the use of my two fiction pieces, "The Baptism of Johnny O'Neill" and "McCarthy Wises Up" first published there in March and October, respectively, 1950.

Especial thanks go also to Bob Sallee, the youngest man in camp in '49, now the only living survivor of the Mann Gulch fire, for permission to publish his remarks at the Mann Gulch Memorial Dedication following these acknowledgments. And I must also thank Earl Cooley for his kind permission to allow me to quote two paragraphs from his excellent book, <u>Trimotor and Trail</u>, in describing the efforts to control the Mann Gulch fire.

And finally, these stories are mainly the experiences of just two of some 250 smokejumpers from the summer of 1949. Each of the others would have equally horrendous stories to tell and adventures to recount. From a bizarre trade come bizarre tales.

I must acknowledge help in gathering these stories and captioning some photos from Chuck Pickard, Jack Mathews, Jerry Linton, Short Hall, and a number of the relatives and friends of the men who died at Mann Gulch. My thanks to all who helped, including the great mountain pilots who took us there.

S.J., San Luis Obispo, 1994

What It Means to be a Smokejumper

Remarks at the dedication of the memorial
to the 13 smokejumpers who died fighting
the Mann Gulch fire, Helena National Forest,
Montana, (made on May 8, 1991 at the
Smokejumper Center, Missoula, Montana) by
Robert Wayne Sallee, the only living survivor
of that August 5, 1949 tragedy.

It is a great privilege to participate in this
dedication. I would like to be able to tell you a lot
more about the men we are honoring today, but in
1949 we trained in 4-man squads. Although you
were a speaking acquaintance to most of the
fellows, you only really got to know people outside
your squad if you were sent out on project work
together.
    Although first-year jumpers made 7 practice
jumps, those with previous experience only made
two, and they were kept in separate barracks from
us. So we had very little opportunity to get to
know them.
    After training we were sent out around the
region on project work. Some together, in fairly
large groups, piling brush and building trails.
Sometimes two or three to augment a ranger
district crew, and sometimes one alone.
    In my case, in 1949, I was sent to the

Canyon Ranger Station on the Clearwater to
replace a man who had not reported for the trail
maintenance crew. We spent most of the summer
as regular Forest employees until Mother Nature
sent a big lightning storm through the region. We
were then called to Missoula as needed and dispatched to fires more or less in the order we
arrived. In my case, except for Walt Rumsey who
was in my training squad, when we were sent to
Mann Gulch all the others were just speaking
acquaintances.

Thus I can't tell you much about them
personally but will try to tell you what kind of
young men became smokejumpers. This was just
after World War II and a lot of returning veterans
were still in college. The competition for jumper
jobs was pretty intense. Earl Cooley and his staff
were looking for young men in perfect health,
athletic in a physical way, although the upper
weight limit of 180 pounds left out the big time
football and basketball players.

Earl and his men wanted experience in the
outdoors and if possible some previous firefighting
experience. So many of the guys had either
worked on blister rust contracts or in brush camps.
I had one summer in a blister rust camp and one
summer on the Kaniksu white pine disease and
stocking survey and had been on several fires in
the Kaniksu.

But most important, when these young men
filled out the application and accepted the job
offer, they demonstrated that they were men who
had decided to test their personal courage---face
fear---fulfill a need to step up from the rest of the

crowd.

When you are a boy growing up, you go
through a series of steps to overcome fear. In the
beginning you are afraid of everything. One by
one you overcome these anxieties until you decide
to put the question of courage aside forever. And
there is no better way than jumping out of an
airplane to convince yourself and show the world
that you are not afraid.

But it isn't easy. The application for the job
isn't too tough because you can always back out
and nobody else will know. But when the job offer
arrives, you know this is for real. "If I keep on
with this, I'm going to have to jump." You lie
awake at night thinking about falling, and eventually those who go on decide, "Yes, I can do it."

And after you report and stand up on the
shock-tower and look down at at least a broken leg
[if things go wrong], you grit your teeth and jump
just like all your buddies are doing.

And when you're kneeling in the doorway of
the plane, looking down at little buildings and
cattle and trees far below, you think, "My God, am
I really going to do this?" Then another fear
comes forth and it dominates your being. And that
is the fear of facing your buddies again if you don't
jump.

So when the spotter hits your leg, you jump-
--and it takes forever to fall that twenty feet or so
to the end of your static line.

I can't describe to you the glorious feeling
that goes with seeing that beautiful white canopy
overhead and the exhilaration of knowing you have
done it. When you reach the ground the comrad-

ery with those who also jumped (in other words, conquered fear today) is overwhelming.

At that moment you become one of an elite group consisting of all those who have jumped before. I won't tell you that there is no concern before the next or future jumps, but they are never like the first one.

I hope I have given you a little insight into what it's like to become a smokejumper. There isn't any other experience like it.

In 1949 the parachute program was still feeling its way. But it was a great success and the proof of that is that it still exists and is needed over 50 years after the first fire jump. There aren't many programs that can match that.

The smokejumping experience has been beneficial in my life and I think the lives of all alumni of the program. Jerry and Rob Linton and I have talked about this at some length, and I think Rob put it best when he told me that after smokejumping everything else was easy. He said even his stint in Korea wasn't as tough.

Smokejumping solidifies a courage that takes you through life. Nothing can ever be as difficult as stepping out that door the first time.

We hear a lot about teamwork in modern life, but there is no better lesson in teamwork than the one you get in checking your buddy's static line and breaker-cords and depending on him to check yours.

Jumpers have a highly developed determination and will to succeed. If you had ever seen a 140 pound man carry 100 pounds of firepack and jump gear up a mountain to the trail because the terrain was too tough for a 1400 pound mule, you would have an understanding of the word determination.

And participating with a crew of jumpers to build a fireline across the head of a fire before it blows up is a study in the will to succeed.

Jerry Linton reminded me that we also came out of the program with a great respect for good health and physical stamina.

I could probably continue this until I had given the program credit for every desirable character trait known to man and maybe the program deserves it. But for myself I feel the greatest benefit was learning how to do a day's work for a day's pay. This program teaches men that if you are given a job, you do it and don't complain. If you don't want it, there are hundreds of others who do. There is no union to protect you. You stand on your own merits and he who works hard succeeds in all things.

Again I want to say I'm sorry I couldn't tell you more about the 13 men we honor today. But I will say this: They were outstanding young men, selected from among the best, with proven courage, determined to succeed and dedicated to doing the job assigned.

They gave their lives trying, and this tribute is long overdue.

[Bob Sallee is now Engineering Manager, Inland Empire Paper Company, Spokane, Washington. Used by permission.]

About the author:

Starr Jenkins, born in Chicago in 1925, is a Cal Poly English professor from San Luis.Obispo, now retired. Before starting his 27 years in college teaching, he taught high school English and history for five years and spent four years in Forest Service information in Albuquerque. While young he worked five summers for the Forest Service in blister rust control, firefighting, smokejumping and air patrol---plus three summers as a ranger in Yosemite National Park. He has a B.A. in history from the University of New Mexico, an M.A. in English from Stanford, and a Ph.D. in American Studies, again from UNM.

His chief works, aside from this book, are: Profiles of Creative Political Leaders (1975); Morelos of Mexico: Man with a Future (a short novel); "Down with Yosemite City," an article in San Francisco Magazine (August 1965); and "How Prop. 13 Could Go National" in the San Francisco Examiner, July 19, 1978.

Starr lives with Stella, his wife for 45 years, in San Luis Obispo, where they both spoil Sara, their elementary-school-age grandchild.

About the photographer:

Peter Stackpole got his start taking brilliant photos of the building of the Golden Gate and San Francisco Bay Bridges, 1934-1937. He was one of the first four LIFE photographers hired by Henry Luce in 1936 to start his great magazine. After a long, spectacular career, Peter lives semi-retired in Novato, a few miles north of San Francisco Bay.

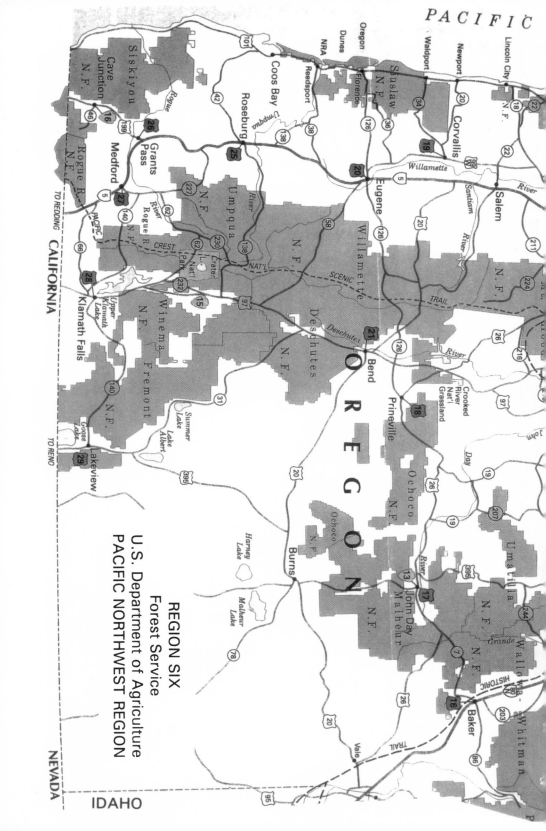

REGION SIX
Forest Service
U.S. Department of Agriculture
PACIFIC NORTHWEST REGION